Purchase, Rehab, and Reposition Commercial Investment Property

Purchase, Rehab, and Reposition Commercial Investment Property

Michael H. Zaransky

KAPLAN PUBLISHING

New York

This publication is designed to provide accurate and authoritative information in regard to the subject matter covered. It is sold with the understanding that the publisher is not engaged in rendering legal, accounting, or other professional service. If legal advice or other expert assistance is required, the services of a competent professional should be sought.

Vice President and Publisher: Maureen McMahon
Executive Editor: Jennifer Farthing
Acquisitions Editor: Michael Sprague
Development Editor: Barbara McNichol
Production Editor: Karina Cueto
Production Artist: PBS & Associates
Cover Designer: Rattray Design

Published by Kaplan Publishing, a division of Kaplan, Inc.
1 Liberty Plaza, 24th Floor
New York, NY 10006

Printed in the United States of America

August 2007

10 9 8 7 6 5 4 3 2 1

ISBN 13: 978-1-4195-9679-7

Kaplan Publishing books are available at special quantity discounts to use for sales promotions, employee premiums, or educational purposes. Please email our Special Sales Department to order or for more information at kaplanpublishing@kaplan.com, or write to Kaplan Publishing, 1 Liberty Plaza, 24th Floor, New York, NY 10006.

DEDICATION

*I dedicate this book to
my supportive parents and in-laws
Roz and Dave Zaransky and
Lily and Jack Mangurten.*

Other Books by the Author

Profit By Investing In Student Housing: Cash In On the Campus Housing Shortage

Writing a book is not a solo effort. A book is an idea that is brought to reality through the hard work and effort of many creative people collaborating together. I love the book publishing process because it is a wonderful collaborative effort that brings a finished product to the readers' hands. It is an honor and a source of great satisfaction to be an author and to quarterback this collaborative process.

I wish to acknowledge former Kaplan Publishing acquisitions editor Vicki Smith for encouraging me to write a second book and for her development of the idea for this work. When Vicki first came to me with the idea of my writing a second book, I was both flattered and nervous. Vickie was instrumental in focusing the theme and ideas for the book and encouraged me to charge ahead with the project. Maureen McMahon, vice president and publisher at Kaplan, signed the publishing contract with me for this book and was a great source for ideas and insight for the direction of the publishing and real estate industries. Maureen has a keen business sense as well as a deep understanding of the real estate business. She is a pleasure to share ideas and conversation with.

My developmental editor, Barbara McNichol, proved herself, once again, to be a true professional and kept me on task and on schedule (well, close to being on schedule, that is). Barbara's finishing touches have made me proud of the final format and content of the book. Without her, this finished book would not be in your hands right now.

My wife and high school sweetheart Barbara continued in her role as my ace proofreader and was constantly encouraging and supportive throughout the process. My children Brad and Karen are the best kids one could ever ask for. Their excitement and pride over this book project makes me smile as I write this acknowledgement. My partner at Prime Property Investors, Ltd., Barbara Gaffen, made many of the examples used in this book possible by partnering with me in a myriad of transactions.

I enjoy writing books about real estate investing because the process merges two of my passions—writing and real estate. I am indebted to the many real estate professionals, bankers, and other advisors that have helped me over the years by sharing their experiences so that I could become successful. I am forever appreciative of the joint venture partners, lending institutions, and investors who have placed their confidence and trust in me over the years.

It is my hope that you, the reader, will find this book useful, and that it will equip you with the tools and confidence to execute deals and profit in the dynamic and unlimited-opportunity world of real estate investing.

—*Michael H. Zaransky*
Chicago, Illinois
2007

Contents

Introduction: Discover the "Rich" Opportunities of Rehabbing and Repositioning Investment Properties   xi

PART ONE

REPOSITION REAL ESTATE BY "MANUFACTURING" DESIRABLE REAL ESTATE

Chapter 1: Four Keys to Repositioning Real Estate Successfully   3
Chapter 2: Increase Your Gross Income   21

PART TWO

EQUITY, DEBT FINANCING, AND FINDING PROPERTY WORTH BUYING

Chapter 3: Equity: What It Is and How to Get It   31
Chapter 4: Debt Financing: Keeping Your Own Cash   47
Chapter 5: How to Find Investment Property Worth Buying   59

PART THREE

REHAB AND REPOSITIONING CASE STUDIES

Chapter 6: Repositioning Single-Family Homes   77
Chapter 7: Repositioning Multifamily Apartment Buildings   89

PART FOUR

OTHER OPPORTUNITIES IN COMMERCIAL AND INVESTMENT REAL ESTATE

Chapter 8: Mixed-Use Repositioning   107
Chapter 9: Net-Leased Properties   111
Chapter 10: Rehab and Repositioning in Retail and Hotels   115
Chapter 11: Real Estate Investment Risk Factors   121
Chapter 12: Choose a Market and Get Started!   127
Conclusion   131

Appendix 1: Sample Condominium Conversion Profit-and-Loss
         Comparison Sheet   133

Appendix 2: Sample Letter to Targeted Investment Property Owners to
         Induce Selling   135

Appendix 3: Sample Cover Sheet for a Resale Marketing Package for a
         Repositioned Apartment Building   136

Appendix 4: Letter of Intent for an Apartment Building or Income-
         Producing Commercial Property   138

Appendix 5: Sample Rider to Form Contract   142

Appendix 6: Due Diligence Checklist for Student Housing   145

Appendix 7: Sample Letter from Developer to Turn Over Management
         to a Condominium Association   148

Appendix 8: Sample Net Profit Projection for a Condominium
         Conversion Rehab and Repositioning Project   151

Appendix 9: Sample Condominium Conversion Unit Purchase
         Agreement   153

Appendix 10: List of Typical Physical Enhancement Improvements for a
         Gut Rehab Condominium Conversion   187

Appendix 11: Sample Income and Expense Projection for an Income-
         Producing Investment Rental Property   189

Appendix 12: Sample Letter to a Homeowner in Foreclosure Seeking to
         Purchase a Home Prior to a Foreclosure Auction   190

Appendix 13: Sample Letter of Intent for a Net-Leased Commercial or
         Retail Property   191

Appendix 14: Sample Single-Family Home Construction Renovation
         Plan   194

Appendix 15: Marketing Page for a Repositioned Single-Tenant,
         Net-Leased Office Building (from a Resale Marketing
         Package)   196

Appendix 16: Sample Return Analysis for the Potential Purchase of a
         Hotel Condominium Unit   198

Appendix 17: Single-Family Home Rehab Project Pro Forma Profit
         Statement   200

About the Author   202

Index   205

DISCOVER THE "RICH" OPPORTUNITIES OF REHABBING AND REPOSITIONING INVESTMENT PROPERTIES

Real estate investment isn't a black-and-white business that opens the door for investors to earn extraordinary profits. Real property values aren't fixed in stone. More than most commodities, real estate values are highly subjective and influenced by a wide variety of factors. As an investor, you'll soon discover that no two pieces of investment real estate are alike. For example, property A may be worth $750,000, while property B, a similar property in type and size, may be worth $1 million. Based on square footage or design style, these two properties are comparable; yet one or more aspects of property B may make it worth $250,000 more than property A.

I've made substantial sums of money first by purchasing commercial and investment properties similar to property A and then by adding attributes and repositioning them to increase their value. In a nutshell, this is the commercial real estate rehab and repositioning business. The concept sounds quite simple. Here's the good news: It is!

MY FIRST SECRET: THE ART AND SUCCESS IS IN THE DETAILS

In this book, *Purchase, Rehab, and Reposition Commercial Investment Property,* you'll learn the details of acquiring commercial and investment real estate, rehabbing it, and repositioning it—capturing the substantially increased value and profits as a result.

By purchasing a piece of real estate in need of rehab or repositioning, you can add value by making changes to a property that makes it worth hundreds of thousands of dollars more. For example, you can capture the increased value, or profit, by reselling the property to another buyer at a gain, or you can keep the property and take advantage of increased cash flow and future appreciation potential. This is my first of many secrets you'll find in this book.

MY SECOND SECRET: THE REAL ESTATE BUSINESS IS BURSTING WITH OPPORTUNITY

I love real estate and the real estate investment business. Real estate is in my blood. I'm the third generation in my family to own and operate real estate investment property actively. Despite the entry of large firms—largely publicly traded Real Estate Investment Trusts or REITs (rhymes with treats) and institutional money investors—real estate remains the turf of individual entrepreneurs. I love that! Although I had a head start using family money to do my first real estate deals, I have many friends in the business who started with absolutely nothing. In fact, it's common to meet multimillionaire property owners who started with no money of their own. Through hard work, they built a net worth of millions of dollars.

Real estate entrepreneurs are fun and creative people. The art of rehabbing and repositioning commercial real estate can be especially creative and rewarding. I get a charge from envisioning an enhanced end product, bringing together all the pieces to improve a property, and reaping the rewards that result. It's a blast to go to work every day and do deals. I'm fortunate to engage in my passion and make money doing it. It's not work—I'm having too much fun! Furthermore, there's a lot of opportunity for profit, and the market is large enough for more players.

I invite you to learn the techniques outlined in this book and join me in this creative—and fun—real estate investment niche.

MY THIRD SECRET: THINK OF THIS AS A "MANUFACTURING" BUSINESS

While much in the real estate rehab and repositioning investment business can be classified as financial- and construction-related, I like to view it as the *manufacturing* business. At its core, this specialized real estate niche manufactures desirable real estate worth much more than the acquisition cost. You "manufacture" the desirable real estate by adding value to the property through improving the physical structure and increasing the attractiveness of the property's physical condition.

You can also improve the financial "structure" of the property by enhancing the cash-flow operating results, and you can reposition the property with a higher market value than it had before you began the value-adding process. In addition, by increasing the gross income generated from a property and/or lowering operating expenses, you can add value and profit from the appreciated fair market value of your real estate investment.

In this book, you'll learn the ins and outs of adding value to a commercial or investment property by making physical and cash-flow enhancements. Specifically, you'll learn:

- how to add value with physical and cash-flow modifications;
- the three necessary elements present in all successful real estate investments: finding equity, obtaining mortgage financing, and finding property worth buying; and
- specific commercial property types ripe for rehab and repositioning profits.

The appendixes provide you with the forms and documents used in actual successful transactions to help you successfully complete profitable rehab and repositioning real estate deals.

I invite you to read on, get creative, and make amazing profits by rehabbing, repositioning, and "manufacturing" commercial real estate investments!

REPOSITION REAL ESTATE BY "MANUFACTURING" DESIRABLE REAL ESTATE

You make amazing profits in real estate by creating *desirable* real estate from *less desirable* real estate. When you add value to a real estate investment you acquire, you create a more desirable property sought by significant numbers of potential buyers. If you have the vision to see how you can reposition a poorly performing or unattractive property, you can capitalize on your vision and make additional profit by creating extra value.

I've found that all value-added property-repositioning techniques fall into one of four general categories. Regardless of the property type, there are four key ways you can reposition and add value to real estate:

1. Make physical enhancements to a property.
2. Master the construction business.
3. Catch the wave of an emerging neighborhood or an upswing trend of a certain type of property.
4. Enhance your net operating income and cash flow from a property.

Most often, you can make physical improvements that result in increased cash-flow potential. In addition, an emerging neighborhood that's becoming a "hot" and desirable place to live creates a shortage of available real estate and, hence, an opportunity to raise rents and increase property cash flow. This is especially true when you invest in apartment buildings in desirable neighborhoods. Sometimes, however, you can create value by enhancing cash flow without making any physical changes to a property. To be a successful repositioning and value-added investor, you'll need to be knowledgeable in all four areas of property enhancement.

1

FOUR KEYS
TO REPOSITIONING
REAL ESTATE
SUCCESSFULLY

In this chapter, we take a closer look at the four keys to adding value and repositioning your real estate holdings.

KEY 1: MAKE PHYSICAL ENHANCEMENTS TO REAL ESTATE PROPERTY

Most investors readily understand that physical enhancements to single-family homes make a house more desirable (thus more valuable) to individual consumers seeking to purchase a home. Most of us have had home-buying experiences. We've found that physically attractive homes are more desirable and valuable than less physically attractive ones. Attractiveness, along with all physical improvements in a single-family home, clearly encourages consumers to pay more for a nicer home. In fact, all my residential real estate agent friends confirm that most homebuyers purchase the nicest homes they can reasonably afford because everyone wants to live in a beautiful home, not an ugly one. Yes, the neighborhood and location are critical in determining the fundamental value in the residential real estate business. However, it's a fact that a nicer, more physically appealing home in the same neighborhood is worth more than a less physically appealing one.

This concept is so obvious that you may be wondering why I even bother to discuss it. Everyone—investors, buyers, and sellers—already know this! I make this point apparent because I've found that the *same principle applies to commercial and investment property*—that is, the more physically attractive properties are worth more than the less physically attractive properties. For some reason, most real estate investors don't believe this and consistently fail to make physical improvements to their commercial property that will enhance value. Keep this in mind, however: The people who buy commercial and investment properties are the same folks who pay more for dolled-up, amenity-rich houses. When buyers of commercial and investment real estate see a physically attractive building, they're willing to pay more for it than for a similar property that's less appealing.

Don't ignore this principle! For some reason, many commercial property owners ignore this simple but true principle of creating real estate value. This creates an opportunity for real estate investors like you to buy less-appealing commercial and investment properties at reduced prices. Then, by enhancing the property, you can increase its value, attract more buyers, and resell your repositioned properties for a profit. It's as simple as that.

Exterior and Interior Improvements

Physical enhancements to commercial and investment property fall into two general categories: exterior and interior. Regardless of whether the physical enhancements are exterior or interior, enhancements can then be either cosmetic or mechanical and structural.

As with residential properties, potential buyers form their first impressions of a property from its exterior physical appearance, known as *curb appeal*. This term comes from the action of evaluating a property and forming an impression based on how it looks while you stand on the curb in front of the property.

In this business, first impressions from the curb clearly set the tone for the desirability and value of a property. In fact, in the residential real estate business, it's difficult to get a buyer to even look at the inside of a house if it has negative curb appeal. In the commercial and investment real estate business, most sophisticated buyers will take a look at the inside of a property and review the financials on a deal regardless of their first curbside impression. However, I can tell you from years of experience that when buyers receive a poor first impression from a neglected or ugly exterior, it raises their antennae, lowers the desirability of the property, and acts as a turnoff instead of creating interest in purchasing the property. Bad curb appeal for a commercial or investment property reduces a potential buyer's desire.

Here's an important key when repositioning investment property: When desire is eliminated or softened, value is lessened. *Less value equates to less profit for you, the seller.*

Cosmetic Changes to Exterior

Types of cosmetic exterior improvements that are fundamental to creating value in any type of real estate include:

- Doing simple routine maintenance
- Keeping the property free of trash and rubbish
- Removing any graffiti
- Maintaining attractive and neatly trimmed landscaping

These simple and inexpensive exterior physical enhancements are so easy to accomplish, yet so often neglected. You'll be pleasantly surprised by how additional exterior cosmetic enhancements can add value to all types of commercial and investment property. These might include adding new windows and trim, having masonry and brick chemically cleaned, replacing old vinyl siding and gutters, painting the exterior so it looks fresh and clean, and adding new or reconditioned exterior doors. New windows, especially on older properties, come with the added benefit of lowering fuel costs for heat, thereby enhancing property cash flow and value.

Of course, when it comes to any rehab and repositioning project, don't get carried away and overspend to enhance the exterior. The extent of the modifications you make and the quality and cost of materials you use should match the neighborhood and property type. For example, don't use expensive mahogany exterior doors when the market will accept lower standards such as an elegant glass or oak doorway system.

Structural Changes to Exterior

Often, it's worthwhile to make mechanical or structural exterior physical enhancements such as replacing or repairing the roof and tuck-pointing masonry. While these physical improvements may not add to the property's cosmetic look and curb appeal, they're perceived in the market as added value—and buyers will pay more for that!

For example, in my experience, buyers will pay more for a commercial or investment property that has a new roof, especially if it comes with a reputable long-term warranty. A new roof, combined with the exterior cosmetic enhancements already mentioned, can reposition a physically undesirable property to the point where its value is significantly enhanced—enough to resell it at a nice and relatively quick profit.

Often in a commercial property transaction, a potential buyer will hire a professional inspector to prepare an engineering report on the property to be purchased. The engineering report is then used by the potential buyer as part of the due diligence to determine if the acquisition makes sense.

When you are selling a rehabbed or repositioned property for profit, you want to make sure that the property will meet a reasonable inspector's scrutiny. I have found that a new roof on a property, particularly one that has a long-term warranty, is so uncommon that it greatly impresses even the most experienced professional inspector. There's nothing better to achieve a positive recommendation in an engineering report than a copy of a contract for a brand new, recently installed roof along with the multiyear warranty that comes with it. The same principle applies to new HVAC systems, windows, plumbing, and electrical renovations. The more you can do to impress an inspector preparing an engineering report, the greater the chance that your contracts for sale will pass due diligence periods and close at higher sales prices.

Cosmetic Changes to Interiors

After the initial positive impression of enhanced curb appeal, the look and feel of the interior adds real value to your repositioning project. Generally, potential buyers notice interior physical enhancements to a property the most. This area also offers the greatest opportunity for creativity.

Naturally, interior physical enhancements require planning and coordination, but be careful to put on the brakes. Virtually unlimited ways exist to spend boundless sums of money to enhance the interior of any type of real estate. The key is to strike a balance—only make the improvements and modifications that are reasonably required to ensure the property is attractive in the marketplace.

The extent that you should enhance the interior of the property varies depending on the type of property you're repositioning. Repositioning a multifamily residential apartment building or condominium will require the most interior enhancements. Buyers are interested in the finished look of the interior living spaces, including appliances, floor coverings, and even paint color, when it comes to residential multifamily properties. The apartment unit will be lived in; it has to look attractive and appealing to the condo owner or tenant to bring the highest possible sales or lease amount.

Repositioning a property that will be used as an industrial warehouse or self-storage facility requires the least interior modifications. Industrial and self-storage properties' value to the end user is in the raw space. It doesn't much matter what color the walls are or if attractive window treatments have been installed. Square footage, ceiling heights, and security are of more concern than interior amenities in industrial transactions. (Later in this book, you'll learn more on techniques to strike the balance between costs and the benefits of enhancements. You'll read about actual, successful rehab and repositioning projects and see how I enhanced the physical interiors of various property types with both modest and aggressive budgets.)

Cosmetic interior physical enhancements aren't cheap. In fact, the sky's the limit when it comes to enhancing a property's interior. Be careful. This is the area in which you're most likely to overspend. Don't put more improvements into a property than the market will recognize in terms of adding value.

Remember, you want increased value that translates into an increased resale price that exceeds the cost of your improvements. *Profit equals cost of the property plus improvements and soft costs minus the resale price.* (Soft costs include interest expense, sales commissions, legal and accounting fees, title insurance, recording fees, surveys, and other miscellaneous closing and transaction costs.)

Hardwood floors are a great value-added enhancer, especially in apartment buildings and residential condominium conversions. Styles, wood types, and finishes vary greatly when it comes to selecting a hardwood floor. It's important to survey the market and provide the type of hardwood floor that the particular neighborhood and end product price point demands. On a 1,500 square-foot condominium unit conversion, for example, an oak hardwood floor might run $7 per foot installed and finished for a total of $10,500. The unit, when completed, could sell for $350,000. If the market expects and is willing to pay for oak flooring, stick with oak floors. Upgrading to cherry wood, or other materials, may bring the installed and finished price to $10 per square foot or $15,000 per unit. On a 10-unit condominium conversion project, switching to cherry wood floors would add $45,000 in total cost.

If the market is only willing to pay $350,000 for a unit with wood floors, it's best to stick with the oak and avoid the temptation to upgrade to cherry wood. You'll make an extra $45,000 by giving the buyer what he or she wants and no more.

When a rehab and repositioning real estate transaction gets into trouble and doesn't make a profit, it's usually because the cost of improvements runs too high. Then you can't command a high enough resale price that would cover the excess costs. I've learned this lesson the hard way. The best way to avoid this pitfall is to resist the temptation to overly improve the interior. Instead, focus on repositioning the look and feel of the property to meet or slightly exceed the quality of similar properties in the same market.

Moreover, avoid adopting the mindset that you're improving the property for your own tastes or desires. You're *not* repositioning the property as you would reposition your own home or office space by adding desired luxuries and amenities that don't add value to the real estate. There's no reason to include a hot tub or swimming pool in the yard of a $250,000 home rehab project in a working-class neighborhood. There's certainly no reason to install marble floors and fountains in a suburban office condominium conversion project.

I suggest constantly looking at other similar, successful, more valuable properties in your local market when you're working on a repositioning project. In addition, you can count on construction supply companies coming out with new, more expensive products. As a result, you'll be tempted to make improvements and compete with other properties that are similar and have higher values. Again, don't push these products—and your budget—beyond what you need for the marketplace.

Cosmetic interior physical modifications run the gamut from new room configurations, flooring, drywall, paint, lighting, window treatments, fixtures, cabinets, and appliances. Of course, all these modifications become much more intense efforts when applied to a residential multifamily development such as an apartment building, town home, or condominium.

On the residential side, you get the most added value putting your attention into kitchens and bathrooms. Even when you reposition industrial and retail commercial projects, you can make many interior cosmetic changes in these two functional areas.

Structural Changes to Interior

Physical interior enhancements that are mechanical or structural in nature include anything that's behind the walls in your repositioning project. While they're not visible to the eye during a property walk-through, these enhancements are important to adding value as well. For example, it's costly to update plumbing and electrical systems in an older, vintage building, but having new systems adds a tremendous amount of resale value to the property. More than that, they take away potential buyers' concerns about any future repair and maintenance costs of old, obsolete systems.

Other examples of mechanical enhancements to interiors that add value include heating, ventilation, and air-conditioning (HVAC) systems; wiring for cable; high-speed Internet; alarm systems; and hot water heaters.

KEY 2: MASTER THE CONSTRUCTION BUSINESS

A key skill to being successful in the rehab and repositioning niche is to master the construction business. Keep in mind that rehab and repositioning investment projects aren't about new construction and building from the ground up. However, other than the foundation and building shell, it's essentially the same business.

You can approach the construction project management process of a rehab and repositioning project in one of two ways:

1. Hire a general contractor (GC).
2. Be your own general contractor.

When to Hire a General Contractor

It costs more to hire a general contractor (GC) than to oversee managing your project yourself, but doing so should give you the expertise you need if you're new to the business. On your first project or two, if you're unfamiliar with construction and how to manage a project, I recommend incurring the extra cost of hiring a GC. The key is to choose wisely. Unfortunately, too many inexperienced or unethical GCs reside in this business.

> **Tips for Selecting a Good General Contractor**
>
> Your first step in sourcing and selecting a GC is to ask other investors, real estate agents, and friends for references. Meet with several general contractors, check their references, make sure they have the required municipal licenses, and verify that they carry adequate insurance coverage.
>
> It is imperative that you get comfortable with the GC you select and make sure he or she owns a respected, reputable firm. Visit completed jobs and talk to past clients before you hire a general contractor. In addition, get advice from your attorney or

insurance agent on the amounts and types of insurance you need to protect yourself both during and after the construction project. Make sure the GC you select carries adequate coverage with highly rated insurance carriers. Also make sure that the GC names you as an "Additional Named Insured" on his or her policy. If there's a problem, you want to be able to deal directly with the insurance company as a named insured rather than with the subcontractor who messed up and caused the problem.

Become Your Own General Contractor

In my rehab and repositioning business, I prefer to be my own general contractor on all projects. This helps me control costs and maximize profit. My company has had the most success when we've taken full control of the construction schedule. By being our own general contractor, we in effect capture the profits that the GC would have made (often the entire profit on the transaction).

If you can master the required skills of the construction management business for small and midsize projects in the $250,000 to $2,000,000 and smaller range, you'll maximize the profits you can make in this niche business. Beware, however; the margins on many transactions simply aren't high enough to justify hiring and compensating a general contractor.

If you decide to become your own general contractor, make sure you follow the advice from your attorney and your insurance broker regarding proper licensing and insurance coverage necessary for retaining an outside third-party GC. Most jurisdictions have no formal requirements for general contractors other than the payment of the licensing fee and providing evidence of proper insurance coverage. Local builder trade associations are a good source of recommendations for general contractor's insurance and local licensing requirements.

Even as a general contractor for your own rehab and repositioning project, you must have adequate insurance coverage.

Make sure you're getting advice from a professional insurance broker with lots of experience with rehab and construction projects. Check out the A.M. Best Ratings of the suggested insurance companies to make sure they're high and acceptable to your potential lenders. In addition, don't take any shortcuts when it comes to local permit requirements. Completing a job with the proper (and legally required) permits and bonds will prevent a potentially larger problem—that is, if you finish it and your lack of permitting is discovered by local building inspectors. Not only is it unethical to skip this requirement, but not obtaining proper approvals can cost you dearly. For example, if your local building department shuts down your project with stop orders, it may make the property itself virtually impossible to resell.

I learned and mastered the construction management business by observing all kinds of construction projects in process. I also read all I could on the topic and enhanced my training with classes through recognized construction industry associations.

If you're already familiar with the construction business, you have a head start for investing in the rehab and repositioning real estate niche. If you're entering uncharted territory, trust me (and I speak from experience), you *can* learn and master this area of expertise.

On the other hand, if you're not willing to commit the time and effort to become proficient in construction management, then the rehab and repositioning real estate investment niche isn't for you. *You simply cannot be successful in this arena without construction management skills!*

I don't mean to make you nervous if you're not the handy, fix-it type of person. In the following chapters, I'll walk you through my proven method to learn the construction management business and, more important, to be successful in this business. I can't hammer a nail straight, and therefore I would never think of messing up a project by trying to do any part of the construction work myself. It's the general contractor's job (soon to be *your* job) to master construction management: *managing* the construction project, not *doing* the actual construction work.

Get into the Field

The first step to learn this business is getting out in the field. Drive to an area of your town where lots of rehab and remodeling work is taking place. Look for the construction dumpsters on the streets or behind active rehab projects. Dress like a contractor (blue jeans and a work shirt) and walk into a building. Take a look at the materials the contractor is using and the project in process. By viewing all types of properties under construction at various stages of development, you'll get a good overview of the nature of the construction business.

New construction projects that aren't far enough along in the process aren't relevant to learning the rehab and repositioning business, so don't waste your time. Once the foundation has been dug and the structure completed, it is considered "under roof" and the interior finishing process is where you have something to learn. Pay attention to finished touches; you can pick up a variety of ideas that way. A unique light fixture, a new-style toilet, or even a paint color can often be discovered by touring project construction sites.

I often pick up names of potential subcontractors by writing down the names and phone numbers on trucks of tradesman at construction sites. If you need a list of working electricians or plumbers in a particular city doing particular types of work, give me a pair of blue jeans, a car, and a yellow pad or paper with pen for an hour. I can easily compile you a list.

Join Trade Associations

Next, join local and national trade associations that provide educational opportunities and reading materials on the construction management and general contracting business. I recommend the National Association of Home Builders (NAHB) and its local chapters. Although the NAHB's primary focus is the residential homebuilding business, its resources and offerings are vast and comprehensive. Local chapters offer courses and seminars geared to all levels of the construction management business. I've found that the principles of residential home construction apply equally to managing construction projects for commercial properties. (Learn more about the National Association of Home Builders at *www.NAHB.org.*)

Your immersion into the construction management business, along with acquiring the knowledge you need to be your own general contractor, can begin tomorrow. You can learn about this business and obtain the skills you need even as you begin searching for property worth buying as a rehab and repositioning candidate.

No matter what level of understanding you have of the construction business, you can always learn more. In fact, I've never stopped studying ongoing construction projects, reading supply publications, learning about new construction materials, or reading about construction management and rehab techniques. It's impossible to know *too much* about construction management.

KEY 3: CATCH AN EMERGING NEIGHBORHOOD OR TYPE OF PROPERTY WHEN IT TRENDS UPWARD

A third key to success is selecting neighborhoods and property types that are ripe for future appreciation in value.

You can reposition a property and add value by purchasing real estate in a location that's currently undesirable but is becoming a more desirable area. By buying and holding a property in a transitional area that is becoming "hot" (where real estate values are appreciating), you can also make a profit by simply holding on and riding the neighborhood wave. Of course, you can make physical enhancements to the property to help increase value, but neighborhood appreciation rates alone will cause appreciation in the resale value even without investing your time and cash to enhance it.

Large urban areas that have growing populations and job growth tend to provide these neighborhood wave opportunities. In my experience, it's much more difficult to find this type of repositioning opportunity in a small town or suburb. However, nearly every large, urban city in America has had a notable, recent upward trend because more people want to live in the city near their jobs rather than commute from the suburbs. This trend, along with overall population and job growth, creates opportunities to profit by buying residential multifamily apartment buildings, retail space, and small office buildings in neighborhoods that are emerging as popular urban locations.

Emerging urban neighborhoods vary from market to market. Discovering where to buy in a particular city requires a good deal of insight into your local market. However, you can look for certain common characteristics when you're choosing an emerging neighborhood. Properties with the following characteristics stack the odds in your favor for appreciation and future profit.

Let's look at three variables: transportation, the Starbucks factor, and hot properties.

Public Transportation Is the Key

Close, convenient proximity to public transportation that moves residents to the central downtown business district is the key to identifying a potential emerging neighborhood. Neighborhoods tend to emerge from the core of the city outward. The hottest neighborhoods with the highest real estate values are found close to the core. Hot neighborhoods move out from the core along the transportation lines. If you look at the train and subway system map of any given city, you can quickly chart the emerging neighborhoods from the core outward.

Watch for the Starbucks Factor

Local shopping at retailers that are desirable to urban residents is important as well. When grocery store chains and popular national retailers move into a particular neighborhood and announce new store openings, take this as a positive sign that the neighborhood is poised to appreciate.

My subjective (and not very scientific barometer) is what I call the "Starbucks factor." In my view, if the highly successful coffee chain opens a new store somewhere outside the core of the central city, that means the neighborhood is about to become even hotter and real estate values are going up. I trust the Starbucks factor because I know the company is doing sophisticated market and demographic research that will show profitable indicators for a store before it ever buys property and opens a store. The same demographic and market factors that make Starbucks open a store in a new neighborhood make me want to own real estate nearby. I expect the neighborhood to have a bright future.

Look for Hot Types of Property

Aside from neighborhood influences, real estate values are often influenced by increases in perceived market value of certain types of property. By buying a particular type of investment real estate when it starts to become more desirable to the real estate investment community, you can reap the benefits of its increased value when you sell the property.

For example, apartment buildings become more desirable as investments when fewer people are buying single-family homes and the home resale market is depressed. When people are not buying homes, they still need a place to live and, in some markets, more consumers are looking for rental apartments.

In another example, self-storage properties become more valuable in areas where people live and work in smaller homes and offices because they need to rent excess storage space. By studying and becoming knowledgeable in real estate trends being accepted in the investment community, you'll be able to purchase a particular type of property when it's gaining acceptance and desirability. After that, you can profit from resale as the market drives the fair market value to a higher price level.

When it comes to tracking trends in real estate property types, the best thing you can do is get active in associations that provide research on the real estate markets and stay current on their publications. You should delve into the research published by the Urban Land Institute (at *www.uli.org*) and the National Multi Housing Council (at *www.nmhc.org*). These two highly professional associations provide some of the highest quality research available.

KEY 4: ENHANCE YOUR NET OPERATING INCOME AND CASH FLOW FROM A PROPERTY

Remember, there are three basic ways to reposition and add value to real estate. Making physical improvements and catching an emerging neighborhood wave are two of the basic methods. The third is enhancing a property's net operating income and cash flow.

When it comes to commercial and investment property, the best way to raise value is to increase your net operating income and cash flow. For example, a property that generates $100,000 a year in net operating income for you is good. However, it's simply not worth as much as a similar property that generates a net operating income of $150,000 or $200,000 a year for you. *It's that simple*. There's no more to this business!

Keep in mind that the point of physically enhancing a property and watching for emerging neighborhoods is to have the *ability* to generate net operating income and receive a greater return on investment for your property. That's how you enhance its fair market value. Of course, it's possible to increase your net operating income and cash flow for a property without catching the wave of an appreciating neighborhood or making physical enhancements to a property. As you'll read later, you can purchase an underperforming property, increase your cash flow, and resell the property at a nice profit *without* lifting a finger to do a single physical improvement.

USING THE FOUR KEYS

By successfully making physical enhancements to a property, mastering the construction business, catching increased neighborhood and property type values, and increasing cash flow, you will make money and increase your net worth in this business. Master the techniques in this book to identify and fund the acquisition of properties worth buying. When you do, you'll be well on your way to making substantial sums of money in the exciting rehab and repositioning property niche.

2

INCREASE YOUR GROSS INCOME

You can increase your net operating income and cash flow for a property by increasing your gross income, lowering your operating expenses, or both.

To increase income, you need to *increase the rental income* you receive when you lease a property. Often, hiring companies to apply a fresh coat of paint, chemically clean exterior brick, and enhance the landscaping are enough to attract a new tenant base willing to pay increased rents.

Making physical improvements will help you command higher rent, but sometimes attracting a new tenant base will do the job without your needing to improve the property. How do you attract tenants who are willing to pay higher rent? One idea is to market a well-located commercial property to national retailers seeking to enter a particular market. Similarly, if you own an apartment building, tenants are often willing to pay increased rent for apartments with washer and dryer hookups and remodeled kitchens and bathrooms.

RAISE THE RENT

Don't forget the obvious: Raise the rent every year. Frequently, long-term property owners fail to raise rents from year to year to stay current with the full market value. These owners pass on modest rent increases (or no increases whatsoever) to their long-term tenants at lease renewal time. It's important always to stay on top of the rental rates offered at competing, comparable properties near yours.

While raising rents from year to year is the goal, the extent of those raises is determined by the market rents for other similar properties. It's nice to figure rent increases based on increased costs or at a certain percentage over current rents, but it's the market that dictates rents, not your own projections. In order to stay at a reasonable level of occupancy, asking rents cannot exceed the market rents at other properties. If the asking rent is too high and lower-priced alternatives are available, you will lose tenants to the competition and have empty (non-revenue-producing) space.

As a new property owner, you may be afraid to raise rents. After all, what if tenants used to paying under-market rents move out and leave the building vacant? In the rehab and repositioning business, it's most often a good thing to have under-market-rent tenants who either take the increase in rents or move out. I would much rather have a vacant desirable space, especially one I can spruce up a bit in order to market to a new, more desirable higher-rent paying tenant. Once the new lease kicks in and cash flow increases due to increased rents, you've added value to the real estate and, indeed, manufactured more desirable real estate! Increase rents in buildings with under-market rents and as leases renew, you increase your net operating income and cash flow.

With this strategy, along with having an increased cash flow, you have an increased fair market value for your property. Remember, the whole point of the rehab and repositioning real estate niche is to increase the fair market value of the property by making changes that enhance value. When it comes to raising below-market rents, be aggressive and don't worry about the possibility of losing low-rent-paying, long-term tenants. Let them walk! Replace them with new, high-rent-paying tenants at market-value rents and increase the value of your property.

LOWER YOUR OPERATING EXPENSES

By carefully monitoring and controlling the operating expenses of your property, you can enhance the net operating income and cash flow, regardless of increases in gross income. Even if the property is fully leased at full fair-market-value rents and there's no opportunity to raise rents, net operating income can be increased by carefully monitoring and reviewing each and every building operating expense, you might be able to cut costs and increase the bottom line. There's almost always some area of building operations that has been neglected or overlooked by the previous owners that, with your attention, can result in lower expenses.

Payroll and Management

In my experience, you can control the overall cost to operate real estate by paying diligent attention to all expense categories and closely monitoring all of your expenses. Hold payroll and management expenses to the minimum required to operate the building efficiently. There's no reason to overspend by having too many employees assigned to a property or paying a costly property management fee to a third-party manager.

Insurance

Closely monitor your insurance costs. While it's important to have adequate property insurance from quality carriers, it's equally important to receive competitive quotes on coverage. I find that insurance coverage premiums vary widely from different carriers and it pays to get multiple quotes for property insurance. I believe in showing loyalty in business, but I don't believe there's value in staying loyal to a particular insurance carrier or broker who doesn't provide competitive quotes. Insurance is a commodity and, as a property owner, treat it as such. Award your business to the lowest reputable bidder.

Repair and Maintenance

Repair and maintenance expenses can vary widely from property to property. A newly rehabbed property should have lower maintenance costs than an older property. In addition, most structural and mechanical physical enhancements result in lower monthly and annual repair and maintenance expenses. Carefully monitor hourly labor costs and seek discounts on parts and materials to lower your overall repair and maintenance costs on newer and older mechanical systems. Take time to get competitive bids for all major repair and maintenance items for every property.

The cost variance between reputable contractors for the same repair job at properties can be amazing. Being too comfortable with the same repair vendor often leads to a creep-up in pricing when vendors know they won't be up against competitive bids for projects.

Utilities

Utility costs are a major and important building expense to monitor closely. Wherever possible, shift the cost of utilities to tenants by passing the cost through as an additional amount due under the lease or by providing separate meters in a building with multiple tenants. Quickly repair any water leaks and dripping faucets to control water expense. Install proper insulation and window seals to control heat costs, and install temperature monitors and timers to control heat expense in properties with a central boiler or furnace system.

Taxes

Another major expense area that requires your attention is real estate taxes. Real estate tax assessment practices vary from county to county, but you must vigilantly review and challenge assessments. Don't simply accept a local assessment authority's method of assessing your property without investigating a potential challenge. There are firms that specialize in making real estate tax assessment appeal challenges on behalf of property owners in every local jurisdiction. It's common for tax assessment consultants to file appeals on a contingency basis in which property owners only pay for results.

USE VIGILANCE

Two identical apartment buildings—with the same gross rental income—built at the same time by the same builder in the same neighborhood can be worth different amounts due to the close monitoring of operating expenses at one rather than the other. If apartment buildings A and B each generate $200,000 in gross annual rents, but because of tight expense controls, building B has $80,000 in expenses while building A has $100,000 in expenses, building B is going to be worth more—perhaps $200,000 to $250,000 more in resale value. The difference could lie in the vigilance of building B's owner's fixing leaky water pipes to lower the water bill, contesting the tax assessment to lower property taxes, and shopping multiple insurance companies to get a lower insurance premium. When building A's owner ignores these cost-saving techniques and becomes complacent, expenses are $20,000 a year higher. An investor is willing to pay $200,000 to $250,000 more for a building that will generate $20,000 more a year over a multiyear, long-term holding period. The market for real estate greatly values the future potential and multiple-year value of increased cash flow. Lower expenses and thereby profit. The market will reward you at least tenfold at the time of the sale!

By increasing gross income and lowering your operating expenses, you can increase your net operating income and enhance your annual cash flow. In doing so, you create value in your property and increase the fair market value of the property. When you reposition a property to provide higher net operating income and cash flow, you can profit by the increased appreciated value of your property.

THE BOTTOM LINE

While all the value-adding techniques work together, the real name of the game when it comes to commercial and investment real estate is the "bottom line." Always keep in mind when you invest in real estate that the bottom line is your net operating income and cash flow. The higher your net operating income and cash flow, the higher the value of the property. Upon the sale or refinancing of the repositioned property, if you have successfully increased your net operating income and cash flow, you will see a nice gain over and above your purchase price and cost of improvements.

To summarize:

- By increasing a property's net operating income and cash flow, you successfully reposition it, which leads to more profit.
- By increasing gross rental income and/or lowering operating expenses, you enhance the overall bottom line profit of a property. The increased cash flow translates into a higher fair market value for the property.
- By increasing gross rents and lowering operating expenses, you increase the potential for profit when you remarket and sell the real estate asset.

Part Two

EQUITY, DEBT FINANCING, AND FINDING PROPERTY WORTH BUYING

Many factors affect the viability of a commercial property rehab and repositioning investment that don't apply to traditional commercial investment real estate properties. For example, additional management, construction, and operational issues in this niche require the attention and diligence of the investor both *before* and especially *after* the property is acquired.

While commercial and investment property rehabs and reposition investments have their distinctions, I've also found similarities to acquiring all types of real estate investments. Whether you're new to investing or a seasoned investor managing large real estate portfolios, you're wise to master three key areas as you close the purchase of any real estate investment transaction.

1. Have equity to invest
2. Arrange financing
3. Find property worth buying

These three areas are so fundamentally important that each warrants its own chapter. Once you've learned to master and control these three areas, you can greatly increase your potential for success and increased wealth in all areas of real estate investing! In particular, you will be on the road to making money by rehabbing and repositioning commercial investment properties.

3

EQUITY: WHAT IT IS AND HOW TO GET IT

When I started investing, I had the lucky advantage of being the third generation in my family to enter the business of buying and owning real estate. Through family partnerships and investments as well as a salary from the family business, I had a fabulous head start. That meant I already had money available to make my own investments. Along the way, the sale of properties that appreciated in value gave me even more available equity so I could increase the size of my investment portfolio and grow my net worth.

COMING FROM WEALTH

If you have access to family wealth, use it to build a strong real estate investment portfolio that will increase your own financial security and provide for generations of your family to come. Having a head start gives you a distinct advantage over those looking for equity to make investments. By investing money prudently, you build on the luck of being born into the right family and the satisfaction of making your own mark.

Yet, even if you weren't born into a "lucky sperm club," you can still be radically successful in real estate. Many people who are multimillion-dollar real estate entrepreneurs today came from ordinary families and started with absolutely nothing. Several others have lost fortunes in their careers and businesses, but made huge financial comebacks in the real estate investment business.

Clearly, the real estate investment field offers anybody with ambition and the ability to have a second (sometimes a third) chance to achieve financial independence and accumulate wealth. I know of no other business that has created as many individual entrepreneur millionaires who started with nothing. In any town, the single largest contributor to the net worth of the wealthiest people is most often the value of their real estate holdings, and when successful family businesses are sold, usually the appreciated value of the company-owned real estate holdings provides their greatest value—more than the operating businesses themselves.

WHAT IS EQUITY?

Have you heard about the "no money down" seminars or read "how to" books for beginning real estate investors? Bookstore shelves and cable television channels have no shortage of "no money down" real estate investment hawkers. Infomercials, seminars at local hotels, and product offerings abound. The hawkers usually promise to turn their buyers into millionaires in a short time by teaching them the secrets of "no money down" real estate investing. The only catch to learning these "secret" techniques is to pay the authors or seminar leaders their fees, upfront of course.

Perhaps the reason these promoters spend so much time holding seminars and doing infomercials instead of buying real estate without money is because they make more money in seminar fees and book royalties than in practicing the techniques they teach!

Here's my take on this: I have been at this business a long time as a third-generation real estate investor. I've served in many leadership positions including the board of directors of a major real estate association. I've also served on a bank's board of directors and loan committees, and I've personally known successful real estate investors. I may have overlooked a "secret" real estate investment technique over the years, but I doubt it. Let me be 100 percent crystal clear on this point—*I have never known or seen a real estate investor who has built a multimillion-dollar real estate portfolio without hard equity money invested in properties.*

Hard Money

Equity is the actual hard money that needs to be invested in a real estate transaction to obtain financing and close a deal. Generally, in the commercial investment real estate field, the required equity investment equals 20 to 25 percent of the purchase price of the property.

The quickest, easiest way to obtain equity and purchase a piece of property is to simply write a check. However, if you don't have enough cash to provide the equity for a transaction don't get discouraged and stop reading this book. My lack of confidence in the "no money down" promoters doesn't mean that your equity must come from your own bank balance. Here's where having a partner may be preferable. Likewise, even if you have the money to make the investment and all of the other pieces can fit together, there are circumstances where you still may want a partner.

Partnership Arrangement

Remember, the real estate business is replete with people who have built up a large net worth even though they started with little or no money of their own. Before you decide that you don't have the equity money available yourself to make the investment, make sure you really don't have hidden equity available. Consider the potential sources of equity you may already have, and note that if you can master the other two key areas for doing a real estate deal—arranging financing and finding property worth buying—but lack the equity, you can always structure a joint venture or partnership to obtain the required equity and get the deal closed. Later sections in this chapter cover partnership arrangements in more detail.

POTENTIAL SOURCES OF EQUITY

Most people who own a residence for any length of time realize an appreciation value in their homes. By tapping into this appreciation value with a home equity loan—the easiest type of financing to obtain—you have cash available to provide the equity for a property purchase. Alternatively, by partnering with a friend or business associate who also has home equity available for investing, potentially you could invest in larger and more numerous investments, too.

Many successful investors, including me, have used home equity loans to establish lines of credit. These provide liquidity and equity when needed to purchase real estate investment properties. Bankers love making home equity loans and, due to their low default rate and potential to grow more customer relationships, they often make interest rates and terms the most attractive of any loan their banks offer.

In fact, even if you don't have an immediate need, setting up a home equity line of credit gives you a low-cost method of creating available equity "firepower" when an opportunity presents itself. Lining up potential equity requirements before an actual real estate investment deal comes your way can give you the confidence and ability to move decisively at the right time.

Borrow on Margin from a Brokerage Account

Depending on your tolerance for risk, another potential source of real estate investment equity is borrowing on margin from a brokerage account. Assuming that you have a brokerage account with a good-sized portfolio of stocks and bonds that you've set up as a margin account, you can draw down a portion of its value, and then use the cash for equity in a real estate transaction.

I'm a firm believer that if you're serious about the real estate investment business, you should have at your fingertips as much equity firepower as possible. You should look for ways to tap into sources like brokerage accounts and be ready with funds in case an opportunity to buy the right property comes around.

Life Insurance Policies

Whole life insurance policies are another potential source of equity firepower. Most whole life policies have a feature that allows the owner to take out a loan against the paid in cash surrender value of the policy. Rates of interest are generally low, but the loan will reduce the amount of the death benefit payout. Taking a loan on a whole life policy is a tax-free way to raise money for a real estate investment and make a potential property acquisition come together. As long as the policyholder remains current on minimum interest payments annually, loans against cash surrender values of life insurance policies never have to be repaid.

Credit Card Lines of Credit

If you have an extremely high tolerance for risk and an appetite for high-cost equity, credit card lines of credit can be another source of equity for real estate property investments (though I strongly recommend against doing this).

I do know a few successful investors who tapped credit card cash advance checks to invest in real estate and started their careers that way. I even know of one investor—one of the smartest people I've met in business—who once used credit card cash advances to pay rent for a downtown Chicago LaSalle Street office. Through that office, he attracted institutional and investor equity money to manage and invest in real estate and venture capital transactions. Today, that investor's net worth exceeds $75 million. He owns a controlling interest in a publicly traded company, and, I am certain, carries no monthly balance on his VISA Card!

THE PARTNER ADVANTAGE

If you want to purchase investment real estate but don't have the required amount of equity money available yourself—or you simply want to share the risk (and reward) of a real estate investment with others—consider taking in partners or forming a joint venture.

I'm also a fan of having active *operating* partners in the real estate business. Knowing that few people are competent in every aspect of running a real estate investment business, I believe bringing in partners with strengths that complement your areas of weakness can be of great value. A partner who is knowledgeable in construction, rehab, and dealing with contractors is particularly beneficial in doing rehab and repositioning transactions successfully. Even if you have enough equity to complete your initial few acquisitions and want to grow the size of your portfolio, you'll need to fund future transactions as well. Sooner or later, you could run out of equity steam. Bringing in partners—especially if they have wealth—can boost your ability to build a real estate investment property portfolio. That's how to supercharge the growth of a real estate empire and each partner's net worth.

"Fall in Love" with a Rich Partner

There's no shame in making money and no reason to disguise your moneymaking motives when pursuing a real estate investment opportunity. To paraphrase a cliché about a materialistic marriage: "When it comes to partners in real estate, why not fall in love with a rich partner instead of a poor one?"

As mentioned earlier, it's important to attract a partner who brings a complementary skill set to the table. Select partners who also have money to bring to the relationship. Remember this: Bringing in partners without money doesn't help you find the equity for purchasing a piece of real estate, but it will cost you a share of the profits and appreciation anyway.

My Partner

My business partner is wealthy, smart, highly educated, and better at details, operations, supervision of others, and management than me. By pooling our talents, collective net worth, and available equity, we have a greater real estate asset value than I could have accumulated on my own. Another advantage: my partner is a woman, Barbara Gaffen.

Unlike the residential sales side of the real estate business, the real estate investment, rehab and repositioning, and acquisition sectors of real estate are dominated by men. Even in the 21st century, women are rarely seen at the negotiating table as principals in commercial real estate transactions. A relatively low number of women are among the ranks of commercial brokerages. Women seem to have made their largest showing of equality on the legal side of the business. In fact, I have noticed that the number of female commercial and investment real estate attorneys involved in transactions I'm part of is increasing. As a result, women who are active in the real estate investment, rehab and repositioning, and acquisition industry *get noticed.*

I encourage aspiring female entrepreneurs to enter this wide-open field. I have not seen widespread evidence of discrimination against women preventing them from advancing in the field; rather, I think the low numbers of women in commercial real estate carries over from years of stereotyping only a few suitable careers for females. None of those stereotypical careers included real estate investing!

Use Your Wealth Wisely

Life can be highly rewarding when you collaborate with other people in a common effort that doesn't include money. I don't at all believe that the purpose of life is to make money, but unlike aspects of my life that involve helping the community and people less fortunate than me, cash is indeed king when it comes to the real estate business. Keep that in mind.

This business should be practiced in a principled and ethical way, also keeping in mind that your goal is to build wealth, not save the world. I hope you use the wealth you build to provide for yourselves and your families as well as contribute to worthy causes that make the world a better place!

OTHER SOURCES OF EQUITY

Aside from your own money and the funds from your active business partner, you can turn to other sources of equity to fund your start-up real estate investment enterprise or provide for the growth of an existing operation. They include:

- Friends and relatives
- Joint ventures

- Syndications
- Institutional partners

Friends and Relatives

Relatives and close friends can be an excellent source of initial equity, particularly for novices getting started in real estate investing. Most people have one or two friends or relatives (or even a greater number) who have money to invest in a real estate transaction. By identifying an opportunity to acquire, doing the legwork, and crunching the numbers, aspiring real estate entrepreneurs can impress friends or relatives, making them inclined to become investors. If they turn you down, don't be a pest, but be persistent and find other potential investors.

When seeking investors, you should remember that people who are affluent like to invest their money, but often have a problem finding opportunities in which to invest. By partnering with them, you can actually help solve the problem of how to invest their extra money. If you can show them your competence at identifying and managing real estate investment opportunities, you will raise the equity you need to do the deal through their participation.

As the buzz spreads within your circle about initial successes, watch for results to snowball. Other family members and friends will want a piece of your action. When that happens, you'll have more sources of equity to do more deals through their equity.

Many large real estate portfolios are owned entirely by groups of family and friends of the initial deal promoter. Depending on the amount of available wealth within your own circle, once you get momentum, you will rarely have to go outside of it to find the equity you need.

Covering Grandma's Interest

A friend of mine, a real estate broker, had little money of his own. One day, he spotted a well-located three-flat apartment building in need of rehab—a diamond in the rough. He went to visit his grandma, a lifelong saver, about being an investor in this project, but when she learned that she had to wait for the complete rehab and resale of the property to see her return on investment, Grandma turned him down flat.

As it turned out, she needed the interest earned on her savings each month to live on. My friend came back to Grandma and offered to pay her the equivalent of six months' worth of interest upfront (a payment he could manage from his meager checking account balance). After agreeing to that, she jumped at the chance to help her grandson get started. A few months later when the property was resold, Grandma made a large return on her investment. Since then, my friend built an investment and building career that has won numerous development awards. He also served as president of his local homebuilders' association, and by the way, became a multimillionaire.

Joint Ventures

Unlike direct partnerships in an operating real estate investment business, joint ventures can be an excellent way to lower risk and share in the required equity for a single or group of real estate investments.

Joint venture strategic alliances with a firm or individual allow real estate entrepreneurs to take on larger transactions or more rapid growth than if you stayed independent. By combining forces, all joint venture partners share in the risk as well as the rewards while contributing only a portion of the equity that would have been needed if the investment were made without a joint venture relationship.

If you reach a point when you see more opportunities than you and your partnership can financially handle, I suggest you form

Choose the Right Joint Venture Partner

As with operating partners, selecting the right joint venture partner is the key. My own company is fortunate to have had several
joint ventures with great partners. These relationships have been
developed over many years. We, and our joint venture partners,
trust each other and work well together. I wouldn't have it any
other way; it's not worth giving up half the deal to a joint venture
partner who is difficult to work with or doesn't carry a fair share
of the workload.

a strategic alliance with a well-capitalized and highly respected
joint venture partner, and then look at reposition and rehab deals
together. Although that would mean giving up half of the cash
flow and upside appreciation, you're getting an extra set of professional evaluation eyes and lots of equity firepower you'd never
have on our own. In addition, if you see more opportunity than
your own pocketbook can afford, it may be wise to make a strategic
decision to give up half of the ownership interest in the deals so
you could deepen your pockets and double your available equity
for investing.

Syndications

Yet another excellent source of equity is through a syndication
of a number of passive investor partners. Syndications, which usually take the legal form of limited partnerships or limited liability
companies, are used for transactions requiring large amounts of
equity. Once a track record has been established, syndications can
be an excellent source of equity from high net worth individual
investors seeking to invest a portion of their assets in real estate.

If you've never syndicated a deal, it is wise to keep a list of
potential passive investors in case you choose to syndicate one in
the future. As anyone in the real estate investment business can
confirm, friends, relatives, contacts, and acquaintances seeking

> ## Sharing the News
>
> Sometimes you have to share bad news with a large group of people who would not be privy to knowing the issues (or mistakes) in your real estate deals if they were not your partners. My experience indicates that sophisticated investors in syndications can accept the news—good or bad—as long as it's presented early and in a clear and concise manner. In the long run, most real estate deals work out fine and investors end up happy and confident—as long as they're kept informed.

investment opportunities often inquire about bringing outside investors into your real estate transactions. The more successful and visible you become, the greater the number of potential syndication contacts you'll have for your list.

The legal requirements, disclosures, and documentation required to raise equity money through syndications are regulated and highly technical. You'll require experienced and prudent legal council to properly prepare the offering memoranda and required disclosures. *Do not skimp on this or take shortcuts.* If you violate the rules, you'll face serious legal consequences.

However, if the deal is large enough and the target group of investors has an appetite for it, syndications can raise large sums of equity capital to make acquisitions and fund the growth of a large real estate portfolio.

You'll find that syndications have their downside. Once you've plunged in and crossed over from using either your own money or money from a small group of friends and relatives, you've entered the world of being accountable to outside partners. Real estate deals rarely work out exactly as projected. Outside investors who have entrusted their money with you have the right to receive reports on the progress of their investment, including periodic financial statements.

Be extremely selective in choosing investors for syndications. I have learned to not solicit money or accept subscriptions for part-

Get On a Syndication Bandwagon

With properties we wish to accumulate and hold long term, my company uses limited liability company syndications to raise millions of dollars in equity capital. If the deal is sound and the promoting partners have the necessary track record and knowledge, large amounts of passive investor money can be available to provide equity for continued acquisitions. We immediately see how investor confidence increases when we put our own hard equity money into each deal. Once you use this syndication method for raising equity successfully, subsequent deals sell out quickly. Naturally, potential investors want to get on a winning bandwagon.

nership units from difficult people or anyone counting on rapid returns of invested funds. These types of investors are simply not worth the almost certain aggravation they will cause.

Instead, ideal candidates for real estate investment syndications are high net worth investors who seek to invest a small portion of their wealth in real estate. They have outside sources of income and can handle the possibility of receiving no distributions from time to time if available cash needs to be reinvested in the building.

Institutional Partners

Institutional investing represents the major leagues of the real estate investment business; there's no quicker way to enter the realm of multimillion-dollar deals and build major real estate empires. Institutional investors include insurance companies, pension funds, and aggregated institutional investor pooled investment funds.

Many institutional investors seek to joint venture with well-established, experienced real estate entrepreneurs for large rehab and repositioning housing deals exceeding $10 million in acquisition price. Large institutions allocate a portion of their massive

What It Means to Be Part of This "Club"

Making the decision to go the institutional investor route sounds alluring. It's definitely like an exclusive "club" that will place you in great company. Entry into this club is limited to those with a proven track record. That means you must have actual transactions under contract that can be underwritten to show high returns using rigorous standards.

Institutional investors tend to dictate "take it or leave it" terms. Preferred returns to the institution are high, combined with minimum rates of return required and short-time exit strategies. Because most of the return on a real estate investment is realized when a property is sold and institutions have stringent rate-of-return benchmarks, to hit the required rate, properties usually must be sold within a five-year time frame. Large rehab and repositioning projects tend to work well within the framework of an institutional investor's parameters. Investors can't hold a property longer if the cash flow is good and future prospects are bright, considering that the institutional investor with a 90 percent equity interest calls the shots.

Additionally, institutional investors retain the right to toss you and your management out of the deal if they are unhappy with the returns. Unlike dealing with limited partnerships or limited liability company syndications, when handling institutional money, you are in control of the deal only as long as you can hit (or exceed) the projections.

assets—billions of dollars a year—for investments in the real estate sector. Because large institutions have little operating and asset management internal abilities, their decision-makers rarely (if ever) buy real estate without joint venture operating partners.

These investors are aware of the positive trends pointing to excellent future prospects through rehab and repositioning investments. They eagerly review proposals for investing their allocated billions into real estate deals.

Investment property portfolios valued in the hundreds of millions to billions of dollars have been built by real estate entrepreneurs using institutional investor money. Having one investor to talk to (instead of the many individual passive partners required in individual investor syndication) is easier and more efficient when putting together a large transaction. Additionally, in the rehab and repositioning housing niche, institutional investors regularly place up to 90 percent of the equity required for the transaction. This limits the promoting real estate investor's equity to 10 percent of the total required.

With institutional money to back you up, your own available equity lasts much longer while giving you control of substantial amounts of real estate assets.

ALWAYS HAVE EQUITY AVAILABLE FOR GOOD DEALS

Given the number of potential sources of equity available to astute real estate entrepreneurs, finding equity should never be a stumbling block to closing a good, solid real estate deal.

Beware: If you have a well-located and properly researched commercial rehab or repositioning deal under contract and you can't get the equity together to close on the transaction, *something must be wrong with the deal.* Take a close look and make sure you're not overpaying for the property or underestimating rehab costs. If you are, start looking for a way out of the contract. Most likely, you've made a serious mistake.

4

DEBT FINANCING: KEEPING YOUR OWN CASH

Once you have the equity required for the down payment on a transaction, you can raise the remainder of the purchase price by mortgaging the property to a lending source. While some investors choose to place large amounts of equity into deals and limit the amount they finance, most investors seek to minimize the amount of equity placed in each deal. They prefer to keep their hard cash available as equity for future transactions.

GET AGGRESSIVE WHEN USING FINANCING

Although my partner and I tend to be conservative in the way we underwrite and calculate potential cash flow on real estate deals, we get aggressive when it comes to using financing. More often than not, we mortgage a property as much as we comfortably can. That said, we never put ourselves at risk of being short on cash flow to cover expenses, provide the money needed to perform the rehab work, or fund a contingency reserve (as well as pay the mortgage). However, we like to save as much equity firepower as possible for the next deal.

A serious real estate investor always looks to the next, not yet unidentified, acquisition. We "deal junkies" secretly suffer from the unfounded fear that we won't have enough money for that impossible-to-pass-up bargain purchase about to cross our desk next month!

Lenders can be a great tonic for this until-now private phobia shared by most real estate entrepreneurs. On good real estate deals with conservative projections, lenders want you to borrow as much as they can lend within acceptable loan guidelines. It's not a mystery why this is so; the more you borrow, the more they earn in fees and interest. In fact, on many occasions, I have found hungry lenders willing to finance transactions and rehab and repositioning projects we've passed on because other buyers relied on unrealistic broker projections or unreasonably low rehab expense budgets and were willing to overpay.

To be specific, most commercial and investment property rehab and repositioning transactions are eligible for between 75 and 80 percent mortgage financing, including both property and rehab costs. To close the transaction and complete the acquisition (after the equity is raised), 75 to 80 percent comes from placing debt on the property to be acquired. As you do more and more rehab and repositioning transactions successfully, more sources of financing will want to lend you money. They like your track record, and because rehab and repositioning transactions tend to be relatively short-term projects, lenders often look for ways to do short-term loans. They then reinvest the loan money in new projects as the older projects are paid off.

Don't Rely on a Lender's Approval to Judge a Deal

Here's my word of caution: When financing a transaction, it's a mistake to rely on a lender's approval to determine if you have enough funds. Doing so is truly a disaster waiting to happen. Particularly in low-interest environments, lenders who eagerly put out lots of money in commercial and investment real estate loans can get too loose with their checkbooks. Be careful. It can be too easy to get into a bad deal when mortgage money to finance 80 percent of a property is readily available.

LENDER RELATIONS

The real estate investment business—more than any business I can think of—is based on forming relationships. Serious investors are never one-time buyers, which makes it even more crucial to build strong relationships.

Unlike a family buying a home once or twice in a lifetime, serious investors growing property portfolios engage in many transactions over the course of their careers. Arranging financing to purchase a principal residence requires almost none of the same skills as arranging for a mortgage on an investment property. There is much more to an investment property financing transaction than meets the eye.

The Importance of Leverage

Financing—called "leverage" in the industry—gives you the financial ability to acquire large amounts of real estate and enhance your overall return on equity.

"Leverage" is to "investment real estate" as "water" is to "fish." If you are in the real estate investment business, you can't make money and grow your portfolio without using leverage. Not surprisingly, the best real estate entrepreneurs and creators of the

Quick, Efficient Access to Financing Is Crucial

I can't overstate the importance of building strong, long-term relationships as a key ingredient to succeed in real estate investing, particularly in this niche. Specifically, there is no greater asset or resource you can cultivate and maintain than ongoing relationships with sources of financing. With mortgage financing representing 75 to 80 percent of the money needed to close a deal, clearly the financing terms can make or break the economic viability of a deal. Therefore, quick and efficient access to that mortgage financing is fundamental to succeeding in this business.

Indeed, without the use of mortgage financing, you have no real estate investment business. Sources of financing are so crucial to your business that you should *never* put all your eggs in one basket. I suggest cultivating multiple sources of financing in case your preferred source stops doing real estate loans or your principal contact leaves for another organization. An active real estate investor can't afford an interruption in reliable, steady flows of mortgage money for new projects.

most wealth tend to have excellent lender relationships and access to the best financing terms available.

When several potential buyers compete for a prime piece of real estate, those who have lined up their financing in advance can outmaneuver their competitors by confidently tying up the property early in the process. When I compete with other buyers for a property (a process I prefer to avoid, but unfortunately often face), I like to stand out from the crowd and make aggressively strong offers. These offers involve more than price. They include these three elements: (1) larger than typical earnest money deposits, (2) shorter due diligence times (more on due diligence in the next chapter), and (3) no mortgage contingency. These elements get the sellers' attention fast.

Lining Up Quick Financing

A few years ago, I was forced to develop a "no mortgage contingency" method of making offers, even on large transactions. This evolved from having to compete for apartment property acquisition deals in hot Chicago neighborhoods where we (and just about everyone else) were hungry for condominium conversions. At this stage in my career, I simply don't need to make my offers contingent on getting a mortgage because I can line up my financing in advance by tapping into my established, informed network of commercial real estate mortgage sources.

My partner and I take pride in the long-standing relationships we've cultivated with local and national banks as well as commercial mortgage brokers. We talk to our bankers frequently, even when we don't have a particular deal under contract. We add lenders and potential new leverage sources soliciting our business to our database for mailings and updates on the status of our business. At least twice a year, we mail information to those on our lenders' database. For example, we send a reprint of an article featuring our company or an announcement of a recent acquisition.

In an attempt to keep our lending rates and terms as attractive as possible, we let our sources know that we deal with multiple sources of financing. We also share the details of transactions with those lenders who did not finance a particular acquisition. That way, they become aware of our activities and realize that they don't have an exclusive on our business. We also facilitate networking with lending sources through our involvement in associations, commitments to civic activities, and membership in chambers of commerce and similar organizations.

Cultivate Lender Relationships

When bankers or other potential lending sources ask me what is new, I take the time to bring them into the process early—and in confidence—on potential acquisitions. I carefully and methodically set them up to *want* to give me millions of dollars for my yet-unknown next deal. For example, by the time our firm decided to enter the commercial and investment rehab and repositioning real estate niche, our current lenders and potential additional sources knew about our plans. They were eager to look at our acquisitions and rehab projects right from the start.

As you do more deals and become more visible in the investment real estate community, you'll find that bankers seek you out. They want to hear about your business plans. I suggest you use quiet times to cultivate lender relationships. That way, you set the stage for quick and positive answers to your future mortgage financing requests.

Through established relationships with lenders, you can prime the pump and get your rehab and repositioning niche mortgage financing source network in place before you ever make an offer on a single property.

MULTIPLE SOURCES OF FINANCING

The widespread appetite for rehab and repositioning deals in the lending community offers further evidence of excellent growth prospects for this category of real estate. The increased availability of mortgage financing serves as a vote of confidence in this niche, giving investors like you greater incentive to commit to this field.

If you are seeking mortgage financing on a well-located, well-researched rehab and repositioning transaction, you're in good shape. Experienced lending sources look favorably on traditional commercial and investment property transactions; they love financing rehab and repositioning deals!

Traditional Bank Financing

Commercial and investment property rehab and reconditioning mortgage loans have long been a preferred product category for both national and local banks that have established commercial real estate lending departments. Banks already active in making real estate loans are receptive to looking at additional opportunities. If they understand the market, most are highly receptive to looking at rehab and repositioning loans. Local branches of national banking organizations and community banks located near the subject property understand this market especially well. Therefore, they can be excellent sources for local property mortgage financing. Because banks are under regulatory pressure to make loans within their local designated credit markets, branches of national bank organizations are particularly receptive to making local real estate loans.

For seasoned real estate investors entering the rehab and repositioning niche, existing bank sources of financing can also be excellent sources. If your own banks have a track record of positive experience with you—and you can show you're familiar with the positive prospects in this niche—you'll find that they welcome the opportunity for increased business. When you present the details of the proposed rehab and repositioning transaction, share the positive value-added opportunities described in this book to help you get a positive response. Especially for your initial deals, you'll see that it's much easier to deal with a banking relationship you've cultivated than start from scratch with a new source.

Working with Small Banks

Small local and regional banks offer quick approvals, continuity of bank personnel, and ease of documentation in getting a transaction closed. As your investment property portfolio grows, however, using these banks exclusively can become a barrier because of their legal lending limits, which are smaller than with large banks. Despite the excellent performance of your loans, at some point in the growth of your real estate portfolio, local and regional banks will reach their legal lending ceiling.

The solution is to use multiple local and regional banks or establish a relationship with one or more large banking companies. With large regional and national banks, you have unlimited lending capacity as well as a wider variety of mortgage loan products often unavailable from small institutions. In fact, a large bank can even offer credit terms at interest rates on loans that are tied to Libor rates, T-bills, or other indexes. That can result in lower mortgage interest rate terms.

Working with Large Banks

On the downside, large banks have a habit of creating too much red tape to complete real estate transactions and get loans funded. Unlike the "on-the-phone first-call approvals" you have come to love from your local community banks, national banks need formal approval from various committees before answering "yes."

In addition, due to consolidations, mergers, and promotions within the national banking organizations, lending officers are constantly being moved to new assignments. Therefore, the relationships you build simply may not last.

RECOURSE FINANCING

Traditional bank mortgage financing from local and regional banks, covering rehab and repositioning projects, is almost always perceived as a negative because their financing on commercial real estate loans (including rehab and repositioning deals) is full recourse financing.

Recourse financing, compared with a nonrecourse loan, requires the personal guarantee of the borrowing entity's individual principals. That means even though the property may be purchased by a limited liability company or limited partnership, you can expect to personally guarantee any deficiency on the mortgage loan in the event the investment doesn't work out and a deficiency balance owed to the bank exists after liquidation.

In most cases, only the active operating partners are required to personally guarantee the mortgage loan. Passive investors (those involved when using syndications) are generally not required to personally guarantee mortgage loans covering the investment property. Indeed, requiring a personal recourse guarantee for passive investors would make raising equity by the syndication method impossible.

My View on Personal Guarantees

I'm not as adverse as other investors to the principle of recourse financing and personal guarantees. Frankly, I don't like having to add up my total contingent liability obligations under personal guarantees covering recourse loans in our real estate portfolio, but I *am* comfortable with the risk. Many seasoned investors I respect strongly disagree with my stance, but I have been at this a long time and have *never once* had to come up with money on an investment as a result of a personal guarantee. I conclude that the likelihood of my personal guarantee being required is so remote that I'm not concerned.

My anecdote to recourse financing with a personal guarantee is to take extra care with the underwriting and risk analysis of all potential acquisitions. That way, I sleep well at night. In addition, we always put enough equity into the deal, making the real risk of a future deficiency above the loan balance remote. If our projections for the deal don't indicate enough cash flow (i.e., there's inadequate coverage for anticipated expenses, rehab and repositioning budget costs, reasonable reserves, and loan payments due the bank), I don't push the deal. I prefer to walk away if I can't buy the property at a price that gives me positive cash flow.

Discipline and Training Required

You'll find it tough to walk away from a well-located property when you get as excited about the overall potential market as I am. It takes discipline and training, but that's what you require to survive in the real estate investment business. I don't rely on rosy projections from brokers or encouraging advice from bankers eager to book another loan. I buy into an old but not overused cliché in this business: "Don't fall in love with a building." Live by those words and you will stay out of financial trouble.

MORTGAGE BROKERS AS SOURCES FOR LEADS

Commercial mortgage brokers can also be excellent sources for potential property leads. Well-connected brokers have vast contacts within the investment ownership and brokerage community, and will often hear about opportunities before they're fully exposed to the market. By educating mortgage brokers on your acquisition criteria, you'll have knowledgeable and well-connected sources of potential deals on your team. Commercial mortgage brokers are not compensated by the hour or retainer; they earn their fees out of the origination fees charged for making the loan. That makes them inexpensive allies to stay in contact with. Your only cost comes out of the origination fees once you've closed on a proposed loan.

Remember, the goal of commercial mortgage brokers is to help you structure a financing transaction at the best possible rate. They want you to close on a loan through them so they can earn a fee from placing the mortgage—and impress you for the next opportunity.

Don't make the mistake of using a residential home loan mortgage broker who claims to have contacts with commercial and investment real estate lending sources. Check out the person's track record and types of recent transactions actually closed by the potential mortgage brokerage firm you are dealing with. It's to your advantage to retain a mortgage brokerage firm that has extensive experience in rehab and repositioning transactions. That way, you can avoid a difficult learning curve and enjoy the benefits of knowing the best financing sources for your niche.

Hire Brokers with Various Funding Sources

Although I'm always a proponent of working with the right individual regardless of firm affiliation, in this area of commercial real estate, be sure to hire the right professional at the right commercial mortgage banking firm. Commercial mortgage brokers are only as good as their sources of financing; therefore the best firms simply have more depth in relationships with willing lenders.

In fact, many commercial mortgage banking firms have direct and exclusive relationships with sources of financing for rehab and repositioning deals that would be unavailable through other mortgage brokers. After successfully closing a few deals, call several commercial mortgage brokers with good reputations and explain your desire to do large rehab and repositioning transactions. The biggest and best mortgage brokers in town will immediately invite you out to lunch!

OTHER FINANCING SOURCES

As rehab and repositioning real estate transactions has become more widely accepted as a niche property class, more lenders have entered the field and now actively seek transactions to finance. In today's competitive environment for loans on highly regarded investment real estate, investors are blessed with heavy competition from lenders for quality deals.

A potential source of mortgage financing for rehab and repositioning transaction is life insurance companies. Accessible through established commercial mortgage brokerage firms, life insurance companies are often an excellent, low-cost provider of debt for commercial real estate transactions. Billions of dollars in life insurance company asset value is placed each year in commercial and investment property mortgages.

THE EASY PART IS OVER

If you've found it difficult to acquire equity and leverage for your new rehab and repositioning niche business, then you'll find that after closing a deal or two, you'll change your mind. If you're a seasoned investor, you'll soon discover that the equity and debt components are the easiest parts of doing an investment real estate transaction. Far and away, the toughest component is finding properties worth buying, particularly in the rehab and repositioning niche.

If you follow the equity raising and leveraging techniques and sources in this book, you won't miss—as long as you have identified a property worth buying. As you'll see in the next chapter, finding that prime property can be challenging. Be prepared; it requires lots of time, effort, and knowledge.

5

HOW TO FIND INVESTMENT PROPERTY WORTH BUYING

Once you've decided to enter the rehab and repositioning investment niche, the toughest part is finding a property worth buying. Yes, it can be easy to locate a piece of real estate available for sale that you envision improving and repositioning, but it can be difficult determining if it provides the potential for a sufficient return and appreciation in value.

Be sure to cultivate lots of patience when it comes to real estate investing! It's impossible to know *when* the right deal will become available for purchase—it requires investigating 10 or more deals to find one that's really worth owning. If you're too eager to enter the game and "pull the trigger" without careful due diligence, you could become the owner of problem real estate. Remember, you need to investigate every opportunity, put together lots of potential rehab and repositioning cost budgets, and inspect dozens of buildings to make this work.

Proceed with caution: The opportunity for cash flow and future price appreciation is so great in the rehab and repositioning investment niche that it is well worth the wait for the right property. Patience is your greatest virtue when it comes to real estate investing.

GET THE WORD OUT

You start by putting the word out that you want this particular asset class of real estate and then get in the game. To be a player in this niche market, begin by becoming a familiar face at the national commercial real estate brokerage companies. These firms become exclusive listing agents at one time or another for rehab and repositioning candidate properties placed on the market across the nation. Most of them have databases of potential buyers for all types of properties. As well, they provide email notification systems for new listings.

If you don't have a direct broker contact at the national firms already, start by perusing company websites to find contact information and join mailing lists. Check with your local real estate brokers' association to find out who are the largest and most active commercial and investment property agents in your area. Many associations have commercial broker divisions and forums with lists of active members.

In addition, in many larger cities, you'll find real estate broker associations that are exclusively for commercial and investment property practitioners. If you check with the National Association of REALTORS®, you can get a list of all of the local real estate associations to start your search.

It's a Local Business

Particularly with small and midsize rehab and repositioning property prospects, the real estate business is a highly local business. In the case of small and midsize properties between $500,000 and $3,000,000 in value, local investors tend to own most of the assets in town. Seasoned real estate investors know the local market and have determined the local players who handle most of the commercial property transactions. If you're new to the business, drive around and look for property managers' names on signs posted on the sides of buildings. Look for on-site management offices in properties in the neighborhood you're considering for investment. Go in and introduce yourself as an investor looking for properties to acquire. Call the management companies in the market and let them know what you're looking for. Send a follow-up letter and card so that they have something on file when they hear of a property that might be for sale. Follow up on property listings and advertisements in the Sunday paper for commercial property sales. You'll quickly determine who the dominant players are. Some of the properties with the best potential are troubled properties in need of rehab. Keep an eye open for properties and owners in trouble. Often cosmetically unappealing buildings with obvious exterior deferred-maintenance issues are great candidates.

By doing a direct mailing to targeted neighborhoods from public records available at the local property assessor you can generate calls from owners who might consider selling. You can also send letters to targeted investment property owners (see example in Appendix 2) to find properties worth buying.

Meet the Principals

After you've identified the major owners and management companies in the local area, make an appointment to meet with one or more of the principals. When you introduce yourself, explain that you're looking for investment opportunities and want to be contacted if they or their clients will be selling the kinds of properties you're looking for. Don't skip this step. It's worthwhile to find out who owns the most desirable rehab and repositioning properties in town.

Networking Pays Off

When we were actively doing rehab and repositioning work in an emerging neighborhood in Chicago, I joined the local Chamber of Commerce and local area builders' group. When I first joined, I sent a letter of introduction and a company brochure to all members and let them know we were interested in making further investments in the community. Other business people saw the value in helping someone who wanted to buy buildings and make improvements in their neighborhood. It would enhance values and the community for everyone with a stake in the neighborhood.

By attending events and networking with other business people in the community—even though my actual office was far away—I was able to establish personal relationships and received many calls about available property acquisitions over the years.

Don't be surprised at how many properties are *not* for sale. Honestly, this is a good sign! Owners must know they have a good thing and can't replace their investment returns after selling their properties. However, you'll find their thoughts may change after a period of time due to estate planning, partner friction, or needs for liquidity. Besides, you're looking for a property in an otherwise good market that isn't performing well because it needs to be rehabbed or repositioned. Strong investment property markets often have few properties on the market for sale.

You do all this because when an owner of a well-located property with potential to rehab and reposition wants to sell, you want to be positioned to receive the first call that person makes.

ESTABLISH CREDIBILITY BY GETTING IN THE GAME

I've found that, no matter how many real estate transactions I've completed or how much access I have to equity and financing, local property owners and brokers give me more credibility if

I've successfully completed a transaction *of any size* in their town. In fact, the first question sellers and local commercial property brokers ask is this: Do you own any other properties near the area? Within a large city like Chicago, owning a property in a particular targeted neighborhood builds credibility with sellers of other properties within that neighborhood. Understand that doing that first deal in a targeted market is critical to doing business long-term in that market.

The first steps toward getting in the game begin by joining a local apartment and commercial property owners' association. Here you can establish local name recognition and gain access to the invaluable mailing list of other members. Next do a mailing to every commercial and investment property owner introducing your firm. State that you're seeking confidential conversations about potential future acquisitions.

Your contacts often put introduction letters in a file when they receive them; but sending them is still worthwhile. They could call you regarding an acquisition opportunity months or years later. At the same time, you're continuing to contact the national and local commercial real estate brokers to let them know you're interested in a particular commercial property niche. Make them aware that you've made an acquisition and want to expand your holdings.

In fact, the advantage of making your first buy in a targeted city or neighborhood is so great that, I must confess, I sometimes pay a bit more than I should or buy a less than superior location property. However, I never go crazy and put myself in a negative cash flow situation just for the sake of getting a toehold in a particular local market or neighborhood.

Take Advantage of the Power of Momentum

I believe in the power of momentum in the real estate business, especially in the rehab and repositioning niche. Your first deal will lead to more investment opportunities and potentially to complete multiple profitable transactions in the same market.

On more than just a few occasions, my partner and I have been contacted directly by other property owners in the neighborhood once they have seen one of our rehab and repositioning projects underway. That's why we always put up a sign with our company name and phone number early in the process announcing the project. Prospective sellers often call to let me know they might be interested in selling. Local tradesman also often call to request being put on the bid list for any of the rehab work that needs to be done.

If you end up overpaying on the first deal, make it a small transaction and use your own money rather than take in outside investors because to continue to raise money for future deals using outside investor money, it's important to maintain a high-rate-of-return track record with syndicated outside-investor deals. Besides, you don't want to be responsible for investor money—or have to answer to others—on a deal that is less than a high return.

When attempting to find a property worth buying, divide the items requiring investigation and due diligence into two categories: factors external to the property and items related to the targeted property itself. Then fully investigate and evaluate both areas to understand the viability of the potential investment.

LEARN ABOUT FACTORS EXTERNAL TO THE TARGETED PROPERTY

Determining the future outlook for growth and development in a particular neighborhood or submarket is fundamental when forecasting the demand for a repositioned property. Simply driving around the area surrounding a potential acquisition candidate will reveal *other* new or rehab developments in the area.

In this business, there's nothing wrong with being a follower. Buildings undergoing improvement and upgrade tend to attract other rehab projects in a community. You can be a pioneer with a great vision for a building located in a blighted area with no attraction for future tenants or property buyers, but it may also leave you stuck with a beautiful improved building in the wrong location.

I always like to get on a train that is already moving in the direction I want to go rather than attempt to start the train moving. In the real estate investment business, momentum created by others isn't something to run away from, it's something to jump on and become part of it.

Rehabbing and repositioning in the right, hot neighborhood can be more important to the success or failure of a project than the quality or attractiveness of the building itself. This is particularly true with multifamily investment properties to be occupied as the principal residence of the ultimate tenants or owners. (You can read about catching the wave of the right neighborhood and the attributes to look for in Chapter 7 on multifamily apartment property rehab and repositioning projects.)

It's important to know that real estate investment is a cyclical business and different property classes become hot and valuable at different times in the cycle. Here are several examples:

- When single-family home sales are off and condominiums aren't being purchased, rental apartment properties tend to be worth more as would-be homebuyers choose to rent instead.
- When the general business economy is off and profits are down, office projects slow and the demand for office space lessens as companies shrink and put off expansion plans.
- When there's excess industrial warehouse space on the market, a rehab and repositioned warehouse project has a

We Received "Good News" Six Months Later

At one point, my partner and I were bullish about a particular college-town market in the Midwest because of the college's growing enrollment and inadequate number of dorm rooms. We had located a student housing property close to campus to buy that needed minor rehab and cosmetic modification. However, we just couldn't get the sellers to come down to a reasonable (but fair) market price.

Six months after the initial negotiations broke down, the sellers' broker called with the "good news" that they were now willing to enter a contract at the price we had been willing to pay. As it turned out, in the interim period, seven other student housing deals were actively being marketed for sale by other owners in the same market. The town was suffering from low occupancy and no rent growth due to a large near-campus apartment building that was offering special lease incentives for the first year. Despite the selling broker's excitement to do the deal at our offer price, we took a pass!

lower chance of success than when the market cycle creates a shortage of available warehouse space.

- When hotel rooms in a particular market are remaining full with high occupancy and daily hotel rates are increasing, there is demand in the marketplace for additional repositioned hotel rooms.

- When there's too much new hotel construction and business travel is slow, it's probably a bad time to start a hotel rehab and repositioning project.

All real estate classes respond to external economic factors in different ways. My advice is to thoroughly research the factors that affect the market niche you plan to invest in. Watch and read everything that influences your selected property class. You will be most successful when you pick one or two niche property classes and specialize in following everything that affects your chosen asset class. Just know that external market factors influence the success or failure of a real estate rehab and reposition project to a tremendous degree. There is no point in fighting the trend. In this business, you want to figure out the economic trend, jump on the hot area, and "go with the flow."

CRUNCHING THE NUMBERS ON A TARGETED PROPERTY

Once you've identified a potential acquisition property, the real work of crunching the numbers to underwrite the deal begins. Do some of that due diligence early on, completing the rest of it only after you've tied up the property at a negotiated price.

Letter of Intent

If you want to move forward with a transaction and take it to a more formal due diligence level, tie up the price with a nonbinding letter of intent signed by the buyer and seller. (See a sample letter in Appendix 4.) Do so in the early stages of the transaction. Of course, if you're new to the real estate investment business, consult an attorney before you draft your letter of intent.

Before we present a letter of intent on a property we might purchase, we do fairly comprehensive financial projections, and unless an unusual circumstance comes up, we make an on-site property inspection. Generally, the broker and/or owner reveal preliminary income and expense numbers and other data about the property. Be sure to make a physical site visit to walk the property. From there, determine a rough idea of the extent of the needed rehab and repositioning work before submitting a letter of intent.

Estimating the Net Operating Income

After reviewing seller-provided numbers combined with our own experience operating other investment properties, we then project a property operating statement for the initial year and following years. Subtracting projected operating expenses from projected income gives us an estimated net operating income (NOI). As we get further into the investigation, we make adjustments to the NOI based on new and better information. In my view, it's impossible to make an intelligent offer on a property without doing preliminary projections and calculating projected net operating income.

In addition to rent, include other potential income items in projected revenue. Calculate also a reasonable amount of vacancy-and-collection loss based on the operating history of the property and other real estate investments in the community. Deduct that estimate from gross revenues to produce an effective gross income forecasted revenue number. Then deduct these projected operating expenses (see Appendix 11 for a list of typical expenses) from the effective gross income to derive the anticipated property net operating income. To summarize:

 Projected gross income – Projected operating expenses = Net operating income

"As-Completed" Value

In examining the potential profitability of a rehab and repositioning real estate investment opportunity, the most important number is the calculation of the "as-completed" value and resulting profit.

A rehab and repositioning property transaction by definition takes a property from where it is today, adds value, and brings it to a new level of value. Doing this repositions the property in the marketplace and creates excess value over and above the purchase price.

By starting with the purchase price and adding in all rehab and repositioning costs, you can determine the total direct improved cost of the property going into it. Once the property is fully improved and repositioned, it will have a new value called the *as-completed value*. The difference between the as-completed value and the initial total direct improved cost of the property will be the gross profit (prior to soft costs) available on the project.

Predicting the final "as-improved" value of a property isn't an exact science and you'll get better at it with experience and successful completion of repositioning projects. Researching the actual market selling prices of similar improved properties within the same market is an excellent way to determine approximate as-completed values. Using professional real estate brokers and licensed appraisers to assist you in determining reasonably accurate as-completed real estate property values are strongly encouraged. The spread between the initial cost and all improvements (as subtracted from the as-completed value of the property) will determine the profitability of the project and determine how much you can pay a seller for a particular property.

Once you've determined the gross profit potential, then you can determine the net profit on a repositioning project by subtracting all soft costs from the gross profit. (Soft costs include interest, closing fees, attorney's fees, and third-party investigative reports.)

SOFT COSTS

Determine the Bottom Line in Rehab and Repositioning

The net profit to be made on a rehab and repositioning real estate investment of any property class can be boiled down to this:

Purchase price + Improvement hard costs = Total going-in property cost

As-completed value − Total going-in property cost − Soft costs = Net profit

Determining and maximizing to your advantage the factors that make up these equations is the entire subject of this book and, indeed, the entire rehab and repositioning real estate investment business. (See Appendix 8 for a sample profit-and-loss comparison for a condo conversion rehab and repositioning project.)

Once you estimate an NOI, total going-in property cost, as-completed value, and net profit, if you still want to pursue buying a particular property given its asking price, arrange for a tour to uncover unpleasant surprises. If you're satisfied with the potential for the building, make your offer by submitting a letter of intent or, depending on the circumstances, submitting a binding contract as your initial offer. In all but a few exceptional situations, reserve a reasonable contingency period of between 7 and 30 days to complete a full due-diligence and feasibility study before your contract becomes binding.

Order Third-Party Investigative Reports

During the due-diligence and feasibility period, do extensive investigations to make sure your income and expense, as-completed value, and improvement cost assumptions will hold up. Consider ordering third-party investigative reports on the property. These reports may include environmental, engineering, mechanical systems, and roof evaluations as well as rehab and construction cost estimates and independent valuation appraisals.

Be sure to coordinate the entire feasibility study process so you can bring in various experts in a timely and logical manner. Have them complete all reports, verifications, and inspections before the contractually stated due-diligence period ends. That way, you have an escape in case you surface discoveries that negatively affect your original NOI or project profit projections.

Take Time to Review Additional Items

While in the due-diligence contingency period on a deal, verify your income and expense numbers by verifying the existence of all written leases covering the term and rental rates projected. Review copies of paid bills and property tax returns and closely inspect the building's physical condition. In addition, review the property for any urgently needed capital improvements, deferred maintenance issues, and appearance upgrades.

When to Make Price Adjustments

If the due-diligence and feasibility reviews turn up bad news that would have a *small* impact on NOI, net profit projections, or required capital investment, I usually let the transaction close anyway. Although one school of thought says, "Play it tough and fight for every dollar to get purchase price adjustments," it's usually not worth the hassle to insist on that. After all, brokers, sellers, and lawyers involved in one transaction usually show up when you're doing transactions in the future. If you become perceived as a tough buyer looking for the last buck, your offer could be avoided in favor of one from more cooperative buyers. I would much rather be perceived as the nice guy (or patsy), especially when doing so costs me little money and positions me to get the first call on the next deal.

However, when your due diligence reveals major problems that will have a *large* impact on NOI, net-profit projections, or increased capital-improvement requirements, you can either walk away from the deal or seek a purchase price concession to stay committed to it. If the adjustment required because of undiscovered or undisclosed issues is too high, it's best to tell the seller you're withdrawing from the contract "pursuant to the feasibility inspection contingency clause" rather than seek a substantial price reduction. In my experience, if the problems you uncover are so great, you're dealing with a dishonest seller who wants to hide problems with the property. It means you'll likely face even more hidden problems in the future.

As a third possibility, if the issues are relatively minor (rather than problems intentionally covered up) and if the deal can still work with a relatively minor price reduction, stay committed to closing in exchange for receiving a price concession. Provided with documentation of problems, reasonable sellers and brokers usually cooperate to work out a price reduction rather than remarket the property. If they hold firm to their price, you have to decide if the deal still makes sense to you.

Make Your Final Evaluation

During this phase, also line up final mortgage financing, put out feelers to raise equity if needed, and check and recheck all your investigations and inspections. If you become uncomfortable with the assumptions used in your projections—the quality of the building, the property's location, the economic environment for the type of property project you're planning, or any aspect that worries you—reevaluate the deal *now* and possibly get out of it. Remember, once the contingency period runs out, the contract becomes binding and you're legally obligated to close, thus putting your earnest money at risk for forfeiture.

LOOK FOR THESE IDEAL ATTRIBUTES

The ideal rehab and repositioning property worth buying includes these attributes:

- Located in a hot neighborhood or city
- Low cost of needed rehab and repositioning improvements
- High demand by end users for this type of property

- High as-completed valuation for property
- Attractive initial purchase price

In the real world, not every property worth buying fits this ideal. Most lack one or more of these ideal attributes. In fact, properties that meet every one of the ideal attributes often attract multiple offers and sell to overzealous and optimistic buyers willing to overpay. Therefore, never forget the discipline required to walk away from a deal that's overpriced. Make sure it provides enough of a net profit or cash-flow potential to cover expenses, contingency reserves, mortgage payments, and a reasonable return on the equity investment.

What to Do When All the Factors Don't Exist

If some of these ideal property attributes are missing, I've found "attractive initial purchase price" trumps all other problems. Obviously, an attractive purchase price alone can't turn a dilapidated slum in a lousy location in need of substantial repair into a desirable high-occupancy building (although, in many cases, if bought cheaply enough, an attractive initial purchase price can overcome these problems as well).

In my experience, this is clearly a business where it pays to buy right. If you overpay for a property, I don't care how many other favorable factors are present, you won't make money. If, however, you buy a property for an attractive enough price, you can overcome lots of negatives and manage to make lots of money.

PUTTING IT ALL TOGETHER

By getting the word out, using the techniques described in this chapter, and establishing credibility, you will, with patience, find property worth buying.

The first deal is often the toughest to find. Once you get a deal or two under your belt and cultivate a reputation for closing on transactions, the word will spread among active brokers and property owners.

Stay with it and always take a look at properties that are presented for review. Most of all, stay in touch with the market and the value of properties. Be on the lookout for underpriced properties; they are rare, but they do exist. If you can buy a property at the right price and improve it by adding value, you will make money!

In the next chapters, you'll learn about the types of investment transactions available to rehab and repositioning real estate investors.

REHAB AND REPOSITIONING CASE STUDIES

We all learn best from concrete real-life examples. In this and the following chapters, you'll read actual case study examples of various rehab and repositioning transactions my company has successfully completed. While I don't claim to know all the answers or to have encountered every type of situation, you'll see a variety of transactions. It's my hope that these examples, which implement many of the principles outlined in previous chapters, will inspire and instruct you in your own repositioning projects.

6

REPOSITIONING SINGLE-FAMILY HOMES

While the clear focus and primary subject matter of this book is the rehab and repositioning of commercial and investment property, I would be remiss if I didn't include a section on single-family homes. There is significant opportunity in most markets for successful rehab and resale of single-family homes. Much has been written on this topic and the rehab and repositioning of single-family homes is often referred to as property "flipping." There are even several nationally syndicated, reality television shows on rehabbing and flipping homes for profit.

I include a section on single-family home rehab not just because it's become popular. It's an excellent way to enter and learn the commercial property repositioning business as well. It's easy to find a single-family home in need of rehab, buy it, finance it, fix it up, and resell it. I always recommend this area as an entry point for young people looking for a career in real estate development or investment. It's a great way to learn the business and get in the game. Within the single-family home rehab and resale niche, it's best to stay within your own metropolitan area where you know the neighborhoods and can easily drive to the property to meet workers and do property showings to prospective end-product buyers. If you're new to the business—or even a seasoned veteran looking to keep your crews busy—start by doing a deal or two in this area. In fact, in the single-family home rehab business, you can start tomorrow—even before you read the rest of this book.

BUYING RIGHT

In today's residential real estate environment, the key to a successful single-family home repositioning project is buying right. By purchasing a home in disrepair or in need of cosmetic updates, you can easily add value and make a profit. Because the overall size of the transaction is relatively small compared to commercial and investment real estate transactions, every dollar really counts. If you're a real estate broker, it pays to join your local multiple listing service (MLS) to gain access to the inventory of available properties, and earn and retain the standard buyer's co-op commission.

I love real estate agents (I've been one for over 25 years and sit on the board of directors of the Chicago Association of REALTORS®) so I hate to cut them out of the picture, but in the case of single-family home rehab and repositioning, if you're a licensed real estate professional, you're wise to act as your own real estate agent and earn the commission split to make the deals work—especially if you don't do the rehab work on your own. In addition to the buy-side co-op commission, you'll be able to list properties in the MLS when you're ready to resell and save the cost of the listing agent's portion of the commission. If you're serious about this business, want to get a deal or two of single-family home rehab under your belt, and aren't licensed as a real estate professional, get licensed—you won't be sorry.

Finding Properties

An excellent source for single-family home rehab and repositioning opportunities are properties in foreclosure. Cultivating relationships with banks, lawyers, and brokers who specialize in foreclosure sale properties is a great way to find deals. In my experience, properties in foreclosure, in addition to having a homeowner in financial problems, are almost always neglected and in need of repair and rehab.

I've found the most effective way to acquire homes in foreclosure is to deal directly with the distressed homeowner. When you contact the owner early in the lengthy foreclosure process, you can often purchase the home, pay off the defaulted mortgage, and give the homeowner some much-needed money. I suggest sending a letter to homeowners with properties in foreclosure. (You can find lists at the local courthouse and often published in the newspaper.) Your letter might generate a few calls from owners looking for a way out of financial trouble. See Appendix 12 for a sample form letter you can use in this situation.

After selecting a neighborhood with fixed-up and improved comparable property sales, you can search the MLS and go to open houses to see the fair-market-value selling prices of fully improved homes. It's important not to overdo improvements. Make the physical enhancements to the property that the market requires and pays for—and no more. How do you know what's appropriate? Spend your weekend going to open houses in the targeted neighborhood to get a feel for market prices and expected amenities.

Upgrading Kitchens and Bathrooms Add Value

Over the course of many years, my company has been involved in the rehab and repositioning of many single-family homes, both detached and attached condominiums. We've done complete gut rehabs with room reconfigurations and all new mechanicals as well as simple and quick cosmetic clean up, in-and-out flips. I can confirm the advice given by most experts and books about home flipping: in this area, remodeled kitchens and baths add value to homes. That means if you're looking to rehab and reposition a single-family home for profit, you have to look at the condition of the kitchen and baths, make improvements that add value, and sell at a price above original cost plus improvement costs. See Appendix 17 for the single-family home pro forma profit and loss statement—it's a great aid in figuring the appropriate level of profitability on a specific potential transaction.

CASE STUDY OF SINGLE-FAMILY HOME COSMETIC REHAB

Cosmetic rehab of single-family homes is the easiest type of rehab and repositioning project to complete and turn over quickly. The problem is the relatively small margins and finding a property worth buying at a low enough purchase price to make a profit. As a general rule, the less value that gets added to a house the lower the purchase price needs to be.

A local real estate attorney who also does estate planning called me one day to tell me of his client's dilemma. His client was looking to place her parents in a much needed skilled-care nursing home but needed the money from their single-family home located in a middle-class north suburban Chicago neighborhood. The problem was that no end-user buyer would be interested in the property because it showed very poorly.

The kitchen was the original 30-year-old model. The cabinets were blue stainless steel, the counter tops were stained and discolored, and there was no dishwasher or working oven. The carpeting was over 20 years old and the unfinished basement frequently flooded. What's more, the client's parents were hoarders (a common trait of immigrant older Americans) and had saved everything they ever owned in the last 30 years. The house was covered with boxes of old useless appliances, tools, and gifts. Two of the

three bedrooms were junk storage rooms with virtuall
the floor visible. Although the house was structurally sound, it was
(to be polite) a total pit!

My lawyer friend used those words that are magic to any property rehabber's ears when he told me, "My client wants to get out quickly and knows she needs to sell the house at a discount." It was time to pounce and I asked to see the house immediately. While I was waiting for the phone call from the client to make the showing arrangements, I looked up the house on the local county assessor's website, saw the official photo, and printed out the property characteristic card with square footage and other important information. This data, along with a glance at a local neighborhood street map, gave me enough information to search the MLS for comparable single-family home sales. The home was in a subdivision of single-family homes all built around the same time by the same builder. As a result, there were many similar models identified by the listing sheet picture of houses recently sold in the same neighborhood. By reading the property amenity descriptions and viewing the virtual tours of those listings, I was able to see the as-completed fixed-up property amenities and ultimate selling prices for similar properties.

By the time I received the call back to arrange the property tour, I knew the market would command a $340,000 resale price for a nicely fixed-up similar style home. When the daughter of the elderly couple called me back to arrange my property tour the next day, I asked her how much she really needed to get out and sell the house "as is." When she responded at $270,000, I knew—based on my knowledge of construction and rehab costs—I would buy the house regardless of the condition I found it in during the property tour. I called the lawyer back the same day, thanked him, and told him I planned to submit a binding contract for an all-cash purchase with no mortgage contingency after I toured the property. While it was important not to seem too eager, I wanted to make sure he didn't make any additional calls to other prospective purchasers.

When I went to the house the next day, I was pleasantly surprised at the excellent exterior appearance. I learned that the daughter had had enough of the old leaky roof and put on a new roof last year, along with building a detached garage in the rear area three years ago. Inside, I was also surprised to see a house in shambles, completely messy with debris in every room. By pulling up a portion of the stained and worn carpeting in a closet area, I noticed oak hardwood floors underneath the carpeting. The basement was a mess, had clear signs of flooding, and even showed signs of mold and mildew, which I was sure to point out to the daughter. I intentionally didn't point out or inquire about the existence of hardwood floors under the ugly carpeting.

While viewing the property, the daughter explained her frustration at the condition of the interior and the fact that her mother and father wouldn't throw out anything. She was overwhelmed at the job she had ahead of her having to clear out the house prior to a closing. She didn't know where or how to begin. When I mentioned that I was in a position to purchase the house completely as is, with all junk "as is" and "where is," her eyes lit up. I knew at that point I'd be able to purchase the house, junk included, for less than her $270,000 asking price. I told her if she accepted my offer, we could close in 30 days and she could take whatever she wanted out of the house, give us the keys at closing, and simply leave everything else.

When I got back to the office, I called the lawyer who referred his client to me. I told him about the poor interior condition and my offer to allow the client to leave all the junk in the house. He had already heard from his client and told me of her excitement and relief at my unique offer. Within an hour, I faxed over a contract with a $255,000 purchase price, fully expecting a counter offer close to the $270,000 asking price. The lawyer called within

20 minutes to say his client had accepted my offer at the $255,000 price. She was on her way to his office to sign the contract.

By listening to the needs and desires of the seller at the property showing, I was able to meet those needs and profit from it. It cost us $2,000 in dumpster and labor costs to completely clear the house of all debris and carpet. I'm sure that I bought the house for $15,000 below the already discounted price because I agreed to take that burden off the seller's mind.

By the way, under the carpet was a magnificent oak hardwood floor throughout the entire house. The wood floor was faded and in need of restaining, but it was in perfect condition, having been covered by carpet for 30 years. Thirty years ago, it was the style to use oak hardwood because then, it was a low-cost floor material. Style changed; it became considered an unfinished look to leave the hardwood floor exposed, so most homeowners covered it with carpeting. My, how tastes change!

Our total construction budget for the house was $40,000. We put in all new kitchen cabinets, counter tops, and shiny white appliances. We hired a waterproofing contractor to seal the leak in the foundation that caused the flooding and finished the basement with drywall and a dropped ceiling. We changed out the toilets and sinks in the bathrooms for new white toilets and wood vanities. The ugly pink bathtub was reglazed white and new ceramic tile was installed in the kitchen and bathrooms.

While we carpeted the basement over the cement floor, we stained the hardwood floors in the rest of the house with a dark rich cherry look. We painted the walls in a beige tone, installed new baseboard trim, and painted it glossy white. We changed the old electrical fixtures with new clean-looking ones, put in a brand new washer and dryer, and replaced the furnace with a brand-new one that had a 10-year warranty. The light switches and outlet covers were changed for white plastic covers and the ugly steel closet doors were thrown in the dumpster and replaced with new white doors. As a finishing touch, we hired a landscaper to trim the bushes in front of the house and planted tulips in the flowerbeds. We spent a total of $42,500 on construction and rehab costs.

Our MLS property listing sheet stressed the all-new and updated rehab of the house featuring the hardwood floors and brand new kitchens and baths. We listed the property at a $349,900 asking price and sold it in two days for $345,000; a net profit of $47,500.

All rehabs don't all work out like this one, but similar deals are out there. The key to cosmetic rehab, as I've stressed, is buying right and getting exposed in the market as an aggressive buyer of homes in need of rehab.

CASE STUDY OF CONDO COSMETIC REHAB

I've also found opportunity in the cosmetic rehab and resale of individual condominiums. Although the market for condominium sales has cooled in most cities and marketing times extended, there is still opportunity for profit if the unit can be bought at the right price. In my own home base of Chicago and many similar cities, a number of high-rise apartment building condominiums were converted in the last 10 years. Often units were sold "as is" with existing 1980s and early 1990s-style kitchens. I've found that units like these in desirable locations lend themselves well to rehab opportunities.

We recently purchased a one-bedroom condominium in a high-rise building in Chicago's Gold Coast neighborhood. This area is the central entertainment area for the city and surrounds the exclusive Michigan Avenue shopping area. A well-kept building, it has a super location with extraordinary views and balconies. The MLS listing for the unit offered it as a bank sale from a lender that had foreclosed on the apartment. The asking price was $215,000 and there was an offer of a 3 percent cooperative brokerage commission. After seeing it, we purchased the unit without hesitation for the full listing price. Other similar units on the same building tier were selling in the $240,000 to $250,000 range.

We spent $8,000 to "doll up" the unit, including all new car-peting, stainless steel kitchen appliances, granite counter tops with a stainless sink in place of the older laminate tops, and a granite top on the bathroom vanity. We put down new, relatively inexpensive but elegant looking base trim throughout the entire unit and painted the walls and trim with a fresh coat of paint. We currently have the property listed for sale at $249,900 and have had several showings. There have been no offers yet, but there's no need to panic. The unit is highly desirable at an excellent entry-level price and our net cost after commission earnings is low for the neighborhood.

SINGLE-FAMILY HOME COMPLETE GUT REHABS

Complete gut rehabs of single-family homes can be costly to complete and take time to rehab and bring to market. (The lon-ger the construction project takes, the greater the soft costs for the project as interest and other holding costs increase.) Vintage homes in desirable and appreciating neighborhoods lend them-selves to complete gut rehabs. There is a growing market, especially in urban neighborhoods, for fully rehabbed and restored vintage homes. Buyers are more demanding as price points increase. Still, profits can be made in the complete gut rehab and repositioning of older vintage-style single-family homes.

A complete gut rehab and repositioning of a vintage single-family home requires a major construction management project and carries a significant amount of risk. The project needs either an outside third-party general contractor or for you to act as your own GC. I wouldn't recommend a complete gut rehab as a first project for someone new to the rehab and repositioning business. That said; if planned correctly and in the right, desirable neigh-borhood, a complete gut rehab can be extremely profitable.

Our company completed a large-scale single-family vintage home gut rehab that won the Chicago Association of REALTORS® Good Neighbor Award due to the positive impact we had on the community with the project. We purchased the 5,000-square-foot, three-level Victorian home for $444,000. Located in Chicago's Lincoln Square neighborhood, this "hot" area was desirable as a place for young professionals to live. It featured trendy new shops—and a new Starbucks. We had just successfully completed a large multiunit apartment building gut rehab condominium conversion blocks away.

Because of our success and reputation in the neighborhood with rehab and repositioning condominium conversions, the real estate agent with the large single-family home listing called with information on the ugly, big old house she couldn't sell. She called it the eyesore of the block, another hoarder-family special. There was a collection of junk, mismatched floors and walls, cracked plaster, and a smelly old basement, no garage, ugly landscaping, and a lack of adequate heat awaiting the buyer of this house. We, of course, knew the neighborhood well. We'd seen $1 million new construction homes being built and sold up the street, and recognized the potential in a complete gut and resale of this "ugly duckling."

So we hired an architect, reconfigured the entire layout of the home, pulled the required permits, and began the six-month-long construction project. After completion, it took a few more months, but we ultimately sold the house for $850,000. With a $250,000 construction/rehab expense over the six-month period, we made a nice profit, improved a neighborhood, and gained pride by receiving an industry award.

The rest of this book and the extensive appendixes deal with our primary focus: the rehab and repositioning of commercial and investment properties. Your move into commercial and investment property repositioning will be a significant leap from the single-family home arena. Compared with single-family homes, it requires significantly greater dollars, more access to capital, and a higher comfort level with financial statement and property income and expense analysis. If you can master the necessary skills, however, the potential for profit is quite substantial and the potential sizes of repositioning projects very large.

Chapter

7

REPOSITIONING MULTIFAMILY APARTMENT BUILDINGS

Multifamily apartment buildings, or *multiunits*, are the bridge between the single-family home rehab and repositioning project and the commercial and investment property repositioning business. Many of the skills and lessons learned from doing single-family home rehab are easily transferable. They form the basis for taking the leap to larger and greater profit (and risk) potential in apartment buildings.

My own passion and the bulk of the money I've made in real estate are in the multifamily apartment building realm. I grew up in the apartment building business—the third generation in my family to own and invest in apartment buildings. I've completed numerous successful apartment repositioning transactions over many years.

Apartment buildings come in all shapes, sizes, and unit mix configurations. Other than a brand-new construction, 100 percent leased at full market rents, fully finished apartment building, it's rare to find a multifamily property that can't be physically or economically improved in some way. As the population continues to grow and jobs continue to be created, I have no doubt that there will always be consumer demand for apartment living. Particularly in most major urban areas, demographics point in the right direction for increased appreciation of the value of multifamily apartment properties. To the extent that a real estate investor can add value to a building, the appreciation trend will be accelerated and increased. This can reap great financial rewards to astute investors like you who buy apartment buildings and enhance value.

MAKING PHYSICAL ENHANCEMENTS TO REPOSITION PROPERTIES: DOING GOOD WHILE DOING WELL

Aurora, Illinois, isn't dissimilar from many towns across the country. Located west of Chicago, the city has a population of approximately 142,000. Much growth and development has occurred due to continued population size increases. Aurora, the third largest city in Illinois, has convenient transportation and access into downtown Chicago. Although it has many submarkets that some consider less than desirable, the main area of the town features tree-lined streets with single-family homes and apartment buildings that remind me of the television town of Mayberry.

When an apartment broker listed a 34-unit vintage apartment building in a largely Victorian single-family home neighborhood of Aurora, I knew we'd be interested in taking a closer look. It turned out the red-brick courtyard-style, three-story walk-up building was located at the gateway to the historic district of the town. Surrounded by single-family homes with large front porches, immense front lawns, with 100-year-old trees lining the quiet streets, the building had no close proximity apartment rental competition. Pulling up to see the property, my partner and I knew it had been neglected for many years. The lawn area was brown and burnt, shrubs weren't well kept, and the white masonry trim accenting the building exterior was badly stained and ugly.

In addition, the common area hallways had chipped and faded paint, missing light bulbs, and cracked windows. The carpeting was filthy and many sections were worn out. The garbage dumpster in the back was too small for the building size and overflowed with debris and boxes. In addition, the hallway smoke detectors mostly hang from a broken thread or were missing completely. I wondered what the exterior and common areas looked like before the owner had cleaned things up in anticipation of showing the property to potential purchasers!

The units themselves were in worse shape. Old, badly discolored flooring, cabinets, and sinks out of *Little House on the Prairie* were the norm for the quality of the kitchens. The bathroom tubs and toilets were old and badly stained, floors were hardwood and scratched and black everywhere, and plaster walls were peeling and cracked in every room of every apartment. As you might have guessed, *we loved it!*

This vintage apartment building in Aurora began as the perfect candidate for a rehab and repositioning project. The rare find—a multifamily apartment building in a growing, desirable residential area—was a perfect candidate for major league, added-value enhancements. Even better, the roof had gotten so bad that the owner, who didn't want to spend money replacing hallway light bulbs, was forced to put on a complete new roof with a 20-year warranty. After a few days of back and forth negotiating over price, the seller accepted our increased offer and we were off and running. I had my moments of doubt when the offer was accepted, unreasonably assuming we had paid too much, but we charged ahead and closed on the transaction within 45 days of the initial contract for purchase.

To be frank, when we purchased the Aurora property, we didn't know what we were going to do with it. It was the only property in that community we had ever bought, the subcontractors were strangers, and the property performed okay in its current state. As we got into the ownership and further review of the market potential to push rents up, it became clear that it would pay to put money into the property immediately rather than wait or do it in phases.

So we cleaned the exterior brick and got the white masonry to sparkle with a special chemical treatment. We planted new grass seed and flowerbeds, and trimmed the bushes. We hired a local landscaping maintenance crew to do weekly trims and clean up. We rimmed the outside of the property with a fence of inexpensive material made to simulate wrought iron. The common area hallways were recarpeted and painted, and new light fixtures and doors were hung. Naturally, we replaced the broken smoke and fire alarms and windowpanes where needed.

Because we hadn't arranged for a major renovation financing line of credit at the initial purchase closing and because our mortgage didn't allow a second mortgage, we were putting lots of cash into the property for capital improvements. We knew the cash flow wasn't returning our money quickly enough. So we slowed down the spending pace and renovated apartments only when they became vacant. Each time we renovated an apartment, we were able to rent it for a large increase.

I learned to never make this mistake again. Now, every time we buy a building, we figure out our plan *before* we close the deal. We arrange upfront for proper financing to execute our game plan *and* our exit strategy. It would have been so much better initially to arrange alternative financing, advancing us the funds to renovate the *entire* building and reposition it at large rent increases quickly.

In addition, our initial thinking was to hold onto the property for an extended period of time. In our haste to close the deal we agreed to a large prepayment penalty if we refinanced the mortgage. Another important lesson was learned: rehab and reposition investment property transactions don't mix with prepayment penalty mortgages. It's better to pay a slightly higher interest rate, or float rather than fix the interest rate and take out a loan that can be paid off at any time in order to sell or refinance when needed.

As the building's gross and net income grew, cash flow improved and we went on to do other major physical enhancements. Our water bill was out of hand and we were constantly repairing busted and leaky old water pipes. The old cast iron pipes were corroded and simply giving out. So we replaced the vertical and horizontal water pipe system with all new copper at substantial cost. Thankfully repair costs, maintenance expenses, and the water bill decreased significantly as a result. Fortunately water pressure, sometimes a slow drip in parts of the building, increased substantially.

Eventually, we found ourselves the proud owner of an absolutely magnificent vintage apartment building in the historic district of a wonderful community. Neighbors and the local city councilman wrote to thank us for investing in the property and enhancing the community. I learned another lesson that I've always carried with me. In the process of doing well for ourselves by increasing the building value and cash flow, we had also done well for the community around us. It felt extremely satisfying and I was proud of my company. In all of our projects, I continue to strive to "do good while doing well." The rehabbing and repositioning business provides a great opportunity to do this!

As a result of our efforts and investment in the apartment building in Aurora, we received the Chicagoland Apartment Association's Vintage Property of the Year Award for the rehab project. It was a great honor that meant a great deal to our company. It had the side benefit of putting us on the rehab and repositioning map in the eyes of the real estate community and potential future property sellers and lenders. In addition, our efforts, our enhancements of the building's physical appearance, and the increases in net operating income and cash flow were financially rewarded when we sold the property at a net profit in excess of $450,000.

MAKING ECONOMIC ENHANCEMENTS TO REPOSITION PROPERTIES

It's also possible in this business to find a property that isn't in need of much, if any, physical enhancement, but is underperforming financially. The number of apartment buildings owned by reasonably capable investors that aren't performing to their full economic potential continues to surprise me. Many properties are rented to tenants at below-market rents— in effect offering a rental rate subsidy to the residents.

In my view, renting an apartment with a fair market rental rate of $1,200 per month for $925 per month is the equivalent of writing a check for $275 per month to the tenant. Most often this situation happens where residents of a building are long-term tenants and the owner has not raised the rents to the market rate each year when the lease expires. In effect, the owner is giving a rent subsidy away of $3,300 over the course of a year. Over a 10-year property ownership holding period, $33,000 is given away on just one apartment. Where under-market rents occur, it always involves multiple apartment units within the building.

New owners are sometimes fearful of raising rent to market rates if the increase is substantial. They often fear that, faced with a major rent increase, long-term tenants will leave, and there will be vacancy expense and loss of revenue until new tenants are found. My experience indicates that most tenants with under-market rental rates know they have a bargain and as soon as they get notice that the building has been sold, they expect to see an increase. They know the free ride is over and are usually not surprised at the renewal lease rate increase.

Where an under-market rental revenue building is available to purchase, there's an opportunity for you in the investment property repositioning niche. When you increase rents to market value and you see a resulting increase in the net operating income and cash flow, you have successfully accomplished after-purchase repositioning. The repositioning and value-added play is pretty straightforward. By buying the building based on the below-market rents and reselling the property based on the new increased market value rents, you can make a handsome profit.

Our company purchased a well-maintained and attractive 24-unit garden-style apartment building in Merrillville, Indiana, located 40 minutes southeast of downtown Chicago. Brought to us by a national brokerage firm specializing in investment property sales, the building was in less than a high-profile or trendy location, but it provided a consistent cash flow and had a high occupancy operating history. Expenses seemed to be under control with all utilities paid by the tenants (individual furnaces and electric service were separately metered and billed to each unit resident).

The deal was relatively small for the national brokerage firm so they had spent little time analyzing the market for apartments in northwest Indiana. Doing our own investigation, we found there had been an influx of potential tenants to the area that was growing and expanding. The commuter rail system from Merrillville to downtown Chicago provided easy transportation for individuals who worked in the city but wanted to live in much quieter (and more affordable) Indiana. Vacancy levels at all apartment buildings in the area were low and rents for similar two-bedroom units were higher at all comparable properties.

We went under contract after some brief price negotiation and closed on the property at a $910,000 purchase price, using 80 percent bank financing. Although we painted the common area hallways, hired a weekly cleaning crew, and added bushes and flowers outside, we stuck to the strategy of repositioning the property by raising rents upon lease renewal. As leases came up, we offered to renew each lease at the full fair market value rent for a 12-month period. Most tenants stayed but some moved. The empty apartments were repainted, made ready, and re-rented at market value to new residents. Two residents who were past due on rental payments were not offered renewals and asked to move out.

After going through a lease cycle and fully renting the building at fair market value rents, the net operating income and cash flow had been gradually increased from our acquisition starting point. We had successfully repositioned the building by adding value in the form of an increased revenue stream. Our efforts were rewarded when we put the property on the market with the enhanced cash flow in place. We sold the building for $1,250,000.

CATCHING THE NEIGHBORHOOD WAVE

More than any other investment property class, multifamily apartment buildings have the potential to appreciate in value based on increases in the perceived value of real estate within the neighborhood. This appreciation, based on location and being in the right place at the right time, results from factors completely external to the property itself. As neighborhoods emerge as "hot" areas (a phenomenon occurring in any growing major American city), apartment properties can increase in value without a single physical or economic enhancement taking place. Real estate investors simply want to pay more because a property is located in a neighborhood that is growing in popularity. The added value isn't found in the building itself; the value-added play is the increased valuation of all real estate in the neighborhood.

Chicago's Rogers Park neighborhood, located on the north side along the lakefront and near the city's north border, is a community with a large supply of vintage apartment buildings. The neighborhood was once a shining gem back in the 1950s and 1960s, boasting of good local public transportation, sandy beaches, and community shopping districts. As the community matured in the 1970s and 1980s, local merchants struggled to stay in business, gang activity became commonplace, graffiti ran rampant, and Rogers Park became regarded as a bad neighborhood. As the tenant base deteriorated, landlords couldn't afford to make improvements and keep their buildings in good shape.

Not unlike many urban-setting neighborhoods when stores were closed and buildings were abandoned, gang activity and crime rates soared. However, there were still groups of people within Rogers Park that cared about their neighborhood. They banded together in community groups with the support of the local police and politicians to reclaim their neighborhood. Slowly but surely, the "good guys" turned the tide and started to win the battle.

In the 1990s and still today, signs of improvement and emerging neighborhood status are all over Rogers Park. Old dilapidated buildings are being bought and rehabbed. Young professionals live in the neighborhood, taking advantage of the beautiful layouts and room sizes in the vintage apartment buildings. The retail areas are being revived and, yes, Starbucks has staked a claim with new stores. The excellent proximity to transportation into the core of the city, along with its magnificent Lake Michigan beaches, has made Rogers Park a renewed, desirable neighborhood with appreciating property values.

Similarly, there are many Rogers Parks all across America waiting for the rehab and repositioning real estate investor like you, with an astute eye for emerging neighborhood trends, to catch the neighborhood wave and profit.

Rogers Park—and the increasing real estate values in the emerging neighborhood—have been good to our company. We have found and completed several apartment building rehab and repositioning deals in the neighborhood. In the last five years, we have made in excess of $1 million in net profits by riding the neighborhood wave in this north side Chicago submarket. In the process, we have improved and restored gorgeous vintage properties and increased the value of the neighborhood for ourselves and others.

It's a self-fulfilling prophecy. Once the neighborhood becomes desirable and investors make building improvements, the neighborhood gets hotter, more investors make more improvements, and so on. An emerging neighborhood adds value on top of the enhancements made to the property and supercharges the rate and extent of appreciation.

Find the "Rogers Park" in your city, use the value-added principles learned in this book, and run with it!

ADDING VALUE AND PROFIT WITH CONDOMINIUM CONVERSIONS

Conversion to condominiums is a great way to add value to a property while capturing the added profit of purchasing the building in bulk and selling it off in pieces for more money than selling it whole. Most Americans choose to own their own homes rather than rent. Condominiums allow people to own their own homes, too, with the advantage of living in an apartment unit setting and sharing common area expenses with other unit owners.

Selling the end product to individual "retail" homeowner consumers involves a complicated process of marketing and selling. It's essential to have expertise in residential real estate sales, whether in-house or hired. Our company acts as its own end-product condominium real estate broker and has developed a unit to handle the sales of our condo development units. The selling-side commissions are substantial; retaining this process in-house adds a good deal of cash flow to the transaction. It's also critical to get expert legal advice from a lawyer familiar with local rules and regulations when taking on any condo conversion project. (See Appendix 9 for a sample condo conversion unit purchase agreement. Appendix 7 is a sample letter from the developer to turn over management to a condo association.)

With all types of rehab projects (as with all property types), there are two categories of condominium conversions: cosmetic and gut rehab. Our company has successfully completed several of both types of condominium conversion projects. Costs and time lines can be substantial and successful projects take a good deal of planning and analysis. (See Appendix 1 for a sample profit-and-loss condo conversion comparison sheet. See Appendix 8 for a sample net profit projection.)

Be aware that doing gut rehabs of apartment buildings to condominiums takes a considerable amount of time to complete and sell. Once the apartment building is purchased for gut rehab, the existing tenants have to be cleared from the building. Then existing leases need to be honored. Because a gut rehab involves demolition and removal of all existing plumbing, electrical, and other mechanical systems, the project really can't begin until the last tenant is moved out.

My advice—based on novice miscalculations early in my career—is to clear the building when all final plans have been drawn up and the city has issued the necessary permits to begin the project. The larger the city, the more complex the construction permit review and the greater the issuance backlog. There's no point getting the building ready for construction by having it empty if permits take months to obtain. During the time you're waiting for city approvals of plans and permits, it's far better to have a stream of income from the existing tenant rental base than no income from an empty building. Trust me on this one; I learned this lesson the hard way.

When it comes to converting residential property condominiums and terminating or not renewing apartment rental leases, you're dealing in an area that's highly regulated by local ordinances. Most jurisdictions have laws requiring tenants to receive advance notice of intent to convert to condominiums and rights

A Lesson Learned

Although we've always been cautious and follow the letter of the law in every respect, I have a good friend in the business who inadvertently messed up on the required notice period for a condominium conversion. When the tenant failed to exercise the right of first refusal, he sold the unit at a nice profit to an eager buyer. When the tenant would not move out, the sale couldn't close and my friend couldn't make the improvements and deliver the unit.

The tenant hired a legal aid lawyer and sued for not giving the required 90-day (instead of 60-day) notice of a right of first refusal. In the meantime, prices of the condominium units went way up and the purchaser of this condominium also sued for the loss of value resulting from the ill-fated closing. It created a big, aggravating mess over a 30-day difference in the notice provision.

To top it off, the tenant had little or no money, poor credit, and in reality, could have never purchased the condominium unit or qualified for financing. It cost my friend over $75,000, plus legal fees and 15 months of delay to settle the litigation and get possession of the unit.

My advice is to follow the letter of the law. If you make a mistake and mess up, settle the litigation by offering a large settlement and move on. It's not worth the legal fees, distraction, and potential negative publicity to dig in and fight in court. In fact, it's far better to pay up early and save yourself time and aggravation.

of first refusal, as well as minimum periods of time before a lease can be terminated or not renewed. Some condominium converters have run into trouble with these requirements. It tied up their projects and created delays for considerable lengths of time. Many incurred substantial fines and penalties. I suggest you proceed with caution, hire a well-informed experienced real estate attorney, and follow the letter of the law in every respect.

After plans and permits are issued, following a well-thought-out construction plan is crucial to efficient completion of the project. It's usually a good idea to improve the exterior of the property and fully build out and finish at least one lower-floor unit as soon as possible while the larger project continues under construction. (See Appendix 10 for a list of typical physical enhancement improvements.) The built-out and finished first floor unit can serve as a model apartment and sales office so that the presale of the project can commence as soon as possible. You can anticipate delays associated with fully completing all units in an apartment building condominium conversion, so don't wait to begin selling the individual units.

Arranging the proper financing before purchasing the property and beginning construction is a "must" in the condominium conversion process. The most common type of financing for a condominium conversion deal is to structure a loan that covers the acquisition of the building as well as the cost of construction and carrying cost during the construction phase. By having the bank obtain an "as-completed" valuation appraisal, a well-capitalized developer should be able to obtain 80 percent financing for the building acquisition and 100 percent financing for the cost of construction. As well, the ability to add to the mortgage balance to cover interest payment costs during the construction period should be included. As units are completed, sold, and closed, partial payoffs of the financing balance are made at each closing. This allows the lender to eventually be paid off in full from the proceeds of condominium unit sales. Once the total financed balance is completely paid off, the condominium converter can retain the full balance of proceeds from the remaining unit sales.

LOOK FOR NICHE OPPORTUNITIES WITHIN A NICHE

Within the multifamily apartment building asset class, there are several subclasses of apartment building types. One particular subclass is student housing properties. Our company is very active in the student housing niche nationwide. My book *Profit By Investing in Student Housing: Cash In on the Campus Housing Shortage*

(Kaplan, March 2006) discusses the opportunities for investors in this rapidly appreciating submarket.

The demographic data compiled by the U.S. Census Bureau makes a case for the continued need for student housing near major university campuses. This triad of factors assures a bright future for well-located student housing properties. They are:

1. Increases in the population turning 18 over the next decade as the Echo Boomer generation reaches college age
2. An increasing percentage of high school graduates enrolling in college
3. Increased budget pressures restricting university spending on new dormitory construction

A large influx of student housing renters will be heading to college campuses. There is no possibility that this trend will be reversed. The die has been cast and you can take advantage of it!

As students become more demanding about amenities and luxury conveniences in student housing apartments, your opportunity as an astute rehab and repositioning investor opens up. This creates a market for the "manufacture" of desirable student housing properties from some of the less desirable products present on college campuses today. You can take older, more rundown campus apartment buildings and rehab and reposition them to realize higher rents and resulting property value increases. Just like the renascences taking place in most American urban centers with the rehab and modernization of in-city vintage rental properties, campus towns are ripe for renovation of older properties as well.

If you have the ability to take an active development role, you'll find real estate opportunities at most major universities to rehab older out-of-date buildings into more modern, amenity-filled (translated: higher rent) apartment complexes. Depending on the condition of the property and the potential for return on investment, options in this area range from simple cosmetic rehab of kitchens and baths and new carpet to full gut rehabs with all new mechanical systems and floor plans.

Student housing transactions are highly specialized and require a good deal of due diligence above and beyond the typical rehab and repositioning project. Aside from evaluating the potential property itself, it's important to analyze the campus and state in which the project resides. (See Appendix 5 for a sample rider of a form contract for a typical student housing transaction. See Appendix 6 for a due diligence checklist for a student housing transaction.)

This isn't an area for the uninitiated or inexperienced, but if you've successfully done rehabs of traditional apartments, you might want to explore rehab opportunities on college campuses. I haven't seen many campus rehabs and repositioning of student housing apartment buildings. Based on my experience in both the student housing niche and rehab and repositioning of apartment buildings in the Chicago market, I sense that the market is ripe for student housing rehab projects on most major college campuses. If an "old beater" apartment building can be bought at the right price, a rehab—and the resulting increase of rents—would add a tremendous amount of value.

Although multifamily apartment buildings provide the most opportunities for rehab and repositioning opportunities and profit, other commercial property types can be rehabbed and/or repositioned in value-added transactions as well. The next section examines and explores those additional commercial and investment property opportunities.

Part Four

OTHER OPPORTUNITIES IN COMMERCIAL AND INVESTMENT REAL ESTATE

As real estate of any property class ages and becomes physically and economically obsolete, you have the opportunity (as an entrepreneur with vision and foresight) to reposition properties and increase your profit. There isn't a single asset class of commercial and investment real estate that doesn't have rehab and/or repositioning opportunities. Within all property types buildings can be purchased, increased in value, and resold at a profit.

You have only to study a particular property type enough to become familiar with trends and values that affect it. Then you'd apply the techniques discussed in this book and successfully reposition the property within the chosen asset class.

Among the property types where I've seen potential for value-added deals are

- mixed-use properties,
- net leased properties,
- retail properties, and
- hotel properties.

8

MIXED-USE REPOSITIONING

A mixed-use property is commonly defined as *real estate that has two or more property types or uses combined in a single building or development.* Most often you'll find properties combining residential use with retail or office use ripe for rehab and repositioning. Usually, the residential component is located on the upper floors, with the retail or office component on the lower floors or at ground level. Retail storefront space with residential above it is an extremely common mixed-use real estate combination in urban areas.

HIGH-GROWTH NEIGHBORHOODS

Older mixed-use properties in high-growth and emerging neighborhoods most often create opportunities for value-added repositioning by physical property enhancements. Newer buildings can be repositioned most often, with value added by changing the economics of the property through increasing gross income and cash flow. As with multifamily real estate, value can be added through rehabbing in either a modest cosmetic manner or a more intense and comprehensive gut rehab project.

As an example, our company completed a successful cosmetic rehab condominium conversion of a mixed-use project in an emerging Chicago neighborhood. It's located in Ravenswood not far from the home of the Chicago Cubs in Chicago's Wrigleyville neighborhood. We purchased a mixed-use, well-located corner property on a main artery street. The building had been fairly extensively rehabbed and renovated by the architect-owner who occupied one of the ground-level storefronts as an office and a large apartment on the second floor above the office.

An earlier property renovation included remodeling most of the apartments on the second and third levels, putting in new windows including the ground-level stores, and adding a building that included two apartments, a large outdoor deck, and an indoor garage. While the building looked attractive from the outside and was structurally sound, the apartments were clearly dated. Two of the storefronts were vacant and one of the ground-level offices was rented at below-market rates. By now, you've guessed it—*we loved it!*

The Ravenswood area was well on its way past the early emerging stages; there were million-dollar renovated homes up the street, easy close proximity transportation, lots of young single and married professionals walking the streets, and oh, yes, a Starbucks one block west of the property. It seemed to us (and we later confirmed) that this property was the perfect candidate for a cosmetic condominium conversion.

At the same time, we were studying an increasing urban-environment trend. As city neighborhoods emerge, renovating and rehabbing increase. Growing numbers of residents want offices near their homes. What's more, a significant number of professionals are owners of entrepreneurial businesses or self-employed service providers such as lawyers and accountants. From these demographic and cultural trends, a new class of real estate is emerging: small office condominiums.

With our construction plan and rehab expectations, we hit the ground running as soon as we closed on the purchase. Unlike a complete gut rehab condominium conversion, a cosmetic conversion doesn't require the complete emptying out of the building. Apartments can be cosmetically rehabbed and sold as condominiums as they turn over without interruption of the income stream from the other rental units.

UPGRADING THE LOOK AND FEEL

The residential part of the project was a breeze. We greatly upgraded the look and feel of the units to meet the tastes of the yuppie neighborhood. By adding a second bedroom to oversized one-bedroom apartments, we added value and increased sales prices just by constructing a wall, door, and closet. We installed hardwood oak and cherry floors, European-style 42-inch kitchen cabinets, granite countertops, and deluxe stainless steel appliances in all the residential units. The bathrooms had the toilets changed out for new ones. Luxurious-looking (but relatively inexpensive) vanities and medicine cabinets replaced the old sinks and discolored mirrors. Bathroom floors were retiled with Italian ceramic tile. New white plastic switch plates and outlet covers were installed in all the condo units. What has become our standard baseboard trim installation and beige walls with white gloss trim paint rounded out the cosmetic renovation of the apartment units. To finish the look and feel, we installed new carpet and added paint in the common area hallways.

Because we did a less costly cosmetic rehab, we were able to market the units at lower sales prices than similar-amenity neighboring gut-rehab and new construction condominiums. The residential condominium units sold out fast, yielding a substantial profit. We paid off financing earlier than projected, thus lowering the carrying costs for the project.

The lower-level storefronts proved to be more challenging. We had assumed, given the neighborhood, we would be able to find quality retail tenants to fill the spaces at market rents. We planned to keep the lower-level retail portion as a long-term income-producing property investment, but parking (or lack of it) did us in. It taught me the necessity of providing adequate off-street and storefront parking to attract retail tenants.

We cleaned up the storefronts, painted the walls, and marketed the ground floor spaces as office condominiums for sale. Sure enough, we sold the spaces to area residents, seeing the advantage of owning their own real estate and becoming investors by owning their own office rather than renting. For a small business owner, the financial advantages of building equity with mortgage payments as well as the tax advantage of the depreciation deduction often makes office condominium ownership a wise investment option.

I like the office condominium business and see it as a wave of the future. Developing office condominiums as a cosmetic condo conversion of existing space can be easy and sweet if you hit the right location and price point. We sold spaces with four white perimeter walls, an HVAC system, and florescent-lighted dropped ceilings, in a local neighborhood on a main street for $170 per square foot. Our combined property purchase and improvement cost was $90 per square foot. Now, that's what I call repositioning real estate and manufacturing value.

9

NET-LEASED PROPERTIES

Net-leased properties are attractive investments, with the most attractive ones highly sought after by savvy real estate investors like you. A relatively passive real estate investment, net-leased properties are usually retail, office, or industrial properties leased to a tenant on a long-term basis with all expenses of the property being the responsibility of the tenant. Triple-net-leased properties—the most attractive type from an investor's perspective—place the obligation of real estate taxes, maintenance, and insurance all on the tenant. The rent payment to the property owner is called *net rent* because it's generally the net amount the owner retains in profit, as there are little or no property-owner expenses.

LONG-TERM NATIONAL TENANT LEASES DESIRABLE

The most desirable net-leased properties in high demand and worth the most are those that have long-term net leases to a highly secure national tenant. If a property is net-leased to a local shoe store with a poor credit history, it will be worth less than a similar property net-leased to a major international firm listed on the New York Stock Exchange. The most common repositioning play, therefore, is to purchase a piece of real estate and obtain a new long-term lease on a triple-net basis from a national firm tenant with a high credit rating. Signing such a lease is a significant value-added enhancement that greatly increases the value of the property without other modifications to the real estate itself.

Today, net-lease properties leased to major national retailers are bought and sold by investors almost as if the stream of income from the lease payments were corporate bonds. The lease obligation of a major national retailer with a high net worth and excellent credit rating is similar to the credit and risk quality of a bond issued by that retailer purchased from a stock brokerage firm. Because net-leased properties with major corporate tenants are deemed as a relatively risk-free and guaranteed payment, the leases are often referred to as "bond-type leases."

The higher the bond credit rating of the tenant is, the more valuable the real estate with the underlying long-term bond-type lease is. Our company has owned net-leased properties rented to the U.S. Postal System (it doesn't get any better in terms of a quality tenant than the U.S. government), major banks, and national New York Stock Exchange Fortune 500 corporations. When the properties we purchased were enhanced with impressive quality net-leases, the value of the real estate to investors escalated overnight. By adding the value of a certain and secure stream of income, we enhanced the economics of the property cash flow and increased the value.

MOST POPULAR INVESTMENT TYPES

If you're a novice in the net-leased property niche, you may be surprised at the extent of real estate assets in the United States that individual and institutional investors own but well-known national names use and occupy as net-leased tenants. Some of the most popular, highly secure, net-leased property investments available today are U.S. post offices, Walgreens, CVS, Starbucks, and Chase or Bank of America branch locations. Having relationships with one or more national firms looking to expand or with their exclusive brokers is an excellent value-added strategy to have when a well-located but empty or under-rented potential location becomes available for sale. If you're active in the net-leased market, you can capitalize by adding to the value of a desirable net-lease and reselling the acquired property at a profit. Appendix 13 provides a sample letter of intent and Appendix 15 has a marketing page for a repositioned single-tenant, net-leased office building, both of which you should find helpful.

10

REHAB AND REPOSITIONING IN RETAIL AND HOTELS

I'm not considered a "retail guy" but I have many friends in the real estate business who actively invest in the retail sector. If you're interested in that niche, you can apply to retail properties the same rehab and repositioning skills of the multifamily apartment building niche (without an eye on kitchens and baths). Look and you'll find opportunities in every major city to purchase run-down, neglected retail strip centers and malls, improve them with physical enhancements, and add value in the process.

On the retail repositioning side of the business, however, you'll need to exercise your skill at attracting quality retail tenants at higher lease rates, which in turn increase net operating income and cash flow. Having well-developed skills and contacts, negotiating well, and identifying the location needs of attractive national tenants leads to success in retail value-added opportunities. If you can physically improve and re-tenant a retail strip center with quality national tenants, you have assured yourself of an asset that has appreciated in value. You will have "manufactured" an attractive investment for the market and will profit on the resale of the asset.

LOOK FOR OPPORTUNITIES WITH HOTELS

At the time of this book's publication, the hotel business is doing very well. Business and leisure travel is experiencing an all-time high. Nationally, hotel occupancy and average daily rates are at historical highs as well. Hotel owners have seen the value of their assets increase substantially. Therefore, a high-occupancy, high-average daily-room-rate hotel is worth a great deal to the real estate investment community. As you might guess, a poor-quality low-occupancy, low-average daily-room-rate hotel is worth a good deal less. By now you probably see where I am going with this scenario. You can appreciate the opportunity of purchasing an underperforming hotel, repositioning it, and reselling at a profit.

DON'T GO IT ALONE

Operating in the complex hotel business demands a great deal of skill and knowledge. It requires more than just access to debt and equity capital to reposition a hotel property profitably. That's why I don't recommend going it alone. Hotel repositioning projects lend themselves well to joint ventures with experienced hotel-industry professionals.

One method of adding value to an underperforming hotel property in a good location is to renovate the property and "reflag" it. In the hotel industry, to reflag a property means to affiliate it with a different chain. Reflagging a hotel property that was run as a local independent to become a licensee of a national chain provides access to national advertising and reservation services. These two factors alone drive customers to the property.

By taking a tired, independent local hotel, renovating it, and affiliating it with a national hotel chain, you can immediately add value that increases the desirability of the property. You have "manufactured" a desirable investment product—a high-occupancy, high-average daily-room-rate hotel.

HOTEL CONDOMINIUMS

A new, less risky, yet specialized way to participate in a hotel investment opportunity has emerged—investment and profit in hotel condominiums. In most major cities, hotel condominium projects—a repositioning value-added opportunity for a hotel property developer—offer an individual investor the opportunity to own a hotel room.

Developers are able to reposition a hotel property in a similar way to purchasing an apartment building, completing a condominium conversion, and selling off individual units at a profit. By purchasing a hotel, possibly reflagging and renovating it, and selling the individual rooms as condos, profits can be made. As is often the case with real estate repositioning, the sum of the parts has a greater value than the whole.

Aside from looking at the potential revenue to be derived from a hotel condominium purchase, it's important to carefully review the condominium declaration and rules and regulations. A project most favorable to investors will fairly rotate the rental of hotel rooms so that none gets preferential treatment when lots of rooms are available. As an investor, I prefer hotel condominium deals in which investors own all of the units and the developer retains none because there's just too much temptation by the developer to rent the house-owned rooms first when other rooms are available.

The value to an investor of a hotel condominium is that it's not like a time share. A hotel condo has all of the attributes of a fee-simple, full-ownership interest; it's not positioned as a right to a set number of days' stay at a property. Hotel condominiums are fully transferable, can be sold at any time, and qualify for traditional second-home and commercial investment property mortgages. When it's being used by the owner, it's not limited as to the number of days and the investor has full access to all of the amenities of the hotel. When it's not used by the owner and placed in the rental pool, it generates money for the owner as rental income minus a management fee.

As room rates increase from year to year, the net operating income and cash flow derived from the ownership of a hotel condominium increase. As we have seen with other types of investment real estate, as net operating income increases, the fair market value of the property goes up as well. Over the long term, hotel condominiums in well-run and desirable hotel locations will greatly appreciate in value.

In selecting a hotel condominium purchase investment—or even contemplating developing a hotel project—carefully complete due diligence and pinpoint the demand for rooms in the city under consideration. Look at citywide hotel occupancy levels. (You can obtain hotel occupancy rates for most cities in America from the local convention and visitor's bureau or the local hotel and motel owners' association.) Consider an occupancy level average of 70 percent or better a good hotel market of opportunity. Make sure, also, that the hotel is a part of a recognized nation chain, or at least part of a well-established worldwide reservation system.

Like typical residential condos, the unit owner has ownership of a room as well as a percentage share in the common elements of the hotel. The revenue derived from the rental of the room, minus a management fee, accrues to the unit owner's account.

As an example, our company found an opportunity in the (still under development) Trump International Hotel at a prime location in downtown Chicago. This real estate niche makes a good deal of sense for both developers and hotel condo unit investors. It's too new to draw a firm conclusion about this trend, but I predict it will grow and hotel condo values will appreciate. Appendix 16 provides a suggested income and expense statement form to use in analyzing the potential return on investment and cash flow from purchasing a hotel condominium.

Chapter

11

REAL ESTATE INVESTMENT RISK FACTORS

It's important for prudent investors to go into the real estate investment rehab and repositioning niche with caution because although the rewards can be great, there are several risk factors to watch out for.

In addition to the construction business-related risks previously discussed, be aware of several real estate industry risk factors. The following ones are present in all types of real estate investing including the rehab and repositioning niche.

GENERAL INDUSTRY RISK FACTORS

As previously indicated, I'm a great cheerleader of the real estate investment business. I can think of no business I would rather be in, and I know many people who have become financially independent multimillionaires in this business.

At the same time, I deplore those who would have anyone believe that the real estate investment business is without risks.

In fact, the only way to stay ahead of its risks is to recognize the potential traps and manage the risk effectively. If you are new to the business, get into it *with your eyes wide open*. If you are a seasoned professional with real estate investment experience, *stay on guard and remain vigilant*.

General Economic Conditions

General economic conditions can have a positive or negative effect on the real estate investment business. The state of the economy affects lenders' appetites for financing, investors' tolerance for equity investments in nontraditional asset classes such as real estate, and consumers' desire to tolerate monthly rent increases. By and large, the traditional residential real estate rental industry is more affected by negative general economic conditions than the rehab and repositioning niche. For example, while traditional multifamily apartment property rent growth and occupancy levels is closely tied to the unemployment rate, rehab and repositioned property rent growth and occupancy don't move with the employment numbers. Generally, the larger the number of people in the workforce is, the higher the occupancy levels and rents in traditional apartment properties are. Job creation does not seem to be a significant factor affecting rehabbed and repositioned property rental rates or occupancy levels. Instead, the occupancy and rent levels of rehabbed and repositioned properties tie more closely to the type and extent of the improvements and "value-added" modifications made at the property.

Favorable general economic conditions are always more desirable and a terrible economy can kill any real estate project. Often, a slowing or sluggish economic environment can be overcome by adding additional improvements and value-added amenities to a rehab and repositioning project.

Rising Interest Rates

Rising levels of interest rates almost always have an effect on the general real estate investment market. Many investment real estate transactions only make sense (based on the purchase price and underlying property cash flow) at lower levels of interest rates on the acquisition mortgage debt. The same real estate investment property transaction may fall apart and not get financed in a higher interest rate environment. Higher interest rate environments require greater net operating income and property cash flow to make lenders comfortable and adequately service the debt.

Residential rental investment properties are a unique real estate asset class that sometimes runs counter to conventional wisdom when it comes to the interest rate environment. When interest rates are low, the alternative to renting an apartment is owning a detached single-family home or a condominium. Consequently, in a low interest rate environment, apartment building vacancy rates run higher and landlords lower rents, often providing incentives to lease their buildings completely. Conversely, when mortgage interest rates are high, fewer people are attracted to home ownership, and fewer consumers qualify for financing, thus increasing the size of the renter pool. With more consumers looking to rent apartments, occupancy levels jump and rents increase. The result is greater net operating income and cash flow for apartment building owners and increased property values *despite* higher interest rates.

Remember, this isn't a simple business!

Competitive Property Risk

All real estate investment property investments subject the building owner to competitive risks of competing properties coming to the market in the same community. Newer and better buildings are constantly being developed and can render what was the number one Class A property an older and tired product. Buying properties below the building replacement cost is a good insurance policy against being one-upped by a shiny new building up the street. The new building owner needs to cover his or her investment with rental rates that support today's construction cost. By acquiring an asset below today's construction cost, you have a competitive rental price advantage to keep your property at a high occupancy level.

Delinquent Rent Collection

The inability to collect rents from tenants in a timely manner is another general real estate investment property risk. It's a fact of life that when people hit hard times and money is tight, they may be slow in paying the rent. Generally speaking, residential rent tends to be paid as a priority. After all, everyone needs a place to live. Therefore, rather than risk eviction, a tenant will pay the apartment rent and skip a payment to the credit card company or other creditors.

In contrast, commercial property tenants can go out of business and bankrupt leaving the property owner with no recourse for collection of past due rent and vacant space to re-rent. Good credit-checking practices and confirmation of employment (in screening tenants in advance of signing the lease) are necessities in order to protect the income stream of a commercial or investment rental property.

Vacant Space

Additionally, all real estate investment properties run the risk of the inability to rent all the available space or meet the projected rental rate objectives. Every investment real estate transaction needs to be underwritten with some reasonable vacancy factor figured in as a cost. It's far too risky to project 100 percent occupancy, even for the best-located investment properties. Undesirable units simply may not rent as quickly or for as high a rental rate as superior units in the complex.

Inability to Control Operating Expenses

While all investors, regardless of experience and sophistication levels, attempt to project future operating expenses for a property, projections are as much art as science. One can never know with absolute certainty what operating expenses will run next year, let alone five years out. Many building operating expenses escalate for reasons beyond the control of the property owner; better management cannot always reduce certain costs. As an example, real estate investors have recently seen substantial increases in heating fuel costs, insurance premiums (a cost that seems to be decreasing at the time this book is being written), and real estate taxes. These couldn't possibly have been quantified a few years ago when building operating cost projections were made.

Government Regulation

An increasing array of government regulations and codes has become the norm in the investment property business. Building and zoning codes may require large expenditures to bring buildings into compliance. Environmental cleanup costs can be hidden and discovered later, requiring a potentially large expenditure. When a property is substantially remodeled, the cost of complying with the Americans with Disabilities Act (ADA) can be staggering. Further, local government registration licensing fees, and inspection costs can add to building operating costs.

Terrorist Risk

In the aftermath of September 11, 2001, a new risk inherent in all real estate investment transactions must be faced up to—the risk of future terrorist attacks in the United States. Terrorist attacks could severely harm the market for and value of investment real estate. Particularly high-profile trophy properties, more likely to be terrorist targets, could become unmarketable without the ability to attract tenants, lenders, or buyers. Future terrorist attacks would also likely drive up the insurance and security costs of all real estate investment properties.

I hate to think or write about the terrorism risk to the real estate investment business. Unfortunately, this risk is very real and needs to be recognized in the 21st century.

Illiquidity of Investment

Finally, a risk that applies to all real estate investment property categories is that real estate remains a relatively illiquid investment. It has become a sought-after investment vehicle for many investors; however, real estate remains a nontraditional asset class without a highly liquid market once the investor decides to exit the business. Unlike shares on the New York Stock Exchange, an investor can't decide to sell out and turn a building into cash with a quick call to a stock broker. Real estate investment property assets take months to market and liquidate.

Knowing and identifying inherent risks in real estate investing shouldn't scare you off from entering the rehab and repositioning niche. It's wise to know potential problems that can hinder your investment up front so you can plan accordingly with a goal of minimizing risk. In my view, the potential profits are so great in the rehab and repositioning business that the benefits far outweigh the risks.

12

CHOOSE A MARKET AND
GET STARTED!

There are countless value-added real estate rehab and repositioning opportunities available within all types of commercial and investment real estate. All you need to do is focus on a particular market and learn what's going on. Stay in touch with neighborhood and property class trends. If you see a certain type of property with certain attributes in a certain location selling for a lot of money, buy one that isn't as nice and make it the same as the higher-priced one. By doing this, you'll increase the value of the property you purchase and be on your way to a career in the rehab and repositioning niche.

As you've seen, properties can be repositioned for profit in a variety of ways. By making physical enhancements to the property, catching an emerging neighborhood trend, and ultimately enhancing net operating income and cash flow, profit can be made in this niche.

When you apply the equity capital and debt-financing principles outlined in Part II of this book, you'll find that funding quality repositioning projects won't be an issue for you. Indeed, the hardest part of the investment real estate business isn't finding the *money* to purchase property; it's finding the *property* that's worth buying.

Use the techniques described throughout this book to find property and then apply the most important ingredient of all—patience. Develop the discipline to walk away from a deal that doesn't make sense or is too much of a stretch (there will be lots of those, so practice walking away early on).

You should start by taking on a single-family home rehab project. It's a great way to learn the business because your initial residential home rehab experiences will give you the foundation to move up to larger, more complicated commercial and investment property deals.

FERTILE GROUND FOR PROFIT

Multifamily apartment property rehab and repositioning opportunities provide fertile ground for profits and will increase your ability to do larger transactions with significant upside potential. Repositioning and resale of rental apartment properties as well as condominium conversions are two more opportunities in this niche. Apartment building restoration and rehab projects also provide the satisfying opportunity to improve neighborhoods. Doing a successful apartment building rehab and repositioning project in an emerging neighborhood gives you a chance to do something good while at the same time doing something well.

Other commercial and real estate investment property types include mixed use, net-leased, retail, and hotel—and this list by no means covers all property types where there is potential to add value and resell at a profit! Aside from actually reselling at a profit, this niche allows you to accumulate a real estate investment portfolio and take cash out of completed projects by refinancing and retaining ownership of the property long term.

CASHING IN WITHOUT RESELLING

Throughout this book, I've referred to the profit opportunity in a successful rehab and repositioning transaction as the *resale of the property at a price above purchase price and the cost of improvements.* I refer to reselling at a profit because it's easily understood. Most often, the way profit is made once a property has been repositioned is through adding value. As we have seen from real-world examples of profitable dispositions, the resale can be either an outright sale of the property to a single buyer, or the property can be divided into pieces and sold off as individual condominiums to multiple end-use buyers.

There is, however, an often-used method to take substantial cash out of a repositioned property without actually selling it. If you become active in the rehab and repositioning real estate niche, I strongly recommend that you *not* resell some of the finished product real estate. Instead, refinance the property and take out the excess financing cash. By increasing the value of an investment property, you enhance the net operating income and cash flow that allows for a new appraisal of the property at a higher valuation than the initial purchase price. Once the increased valuation can be documented, a new loan for a higher amount can be taken out on the property paying off the old lower amount of indebtedness and leaving a balance for you. When you do this, you build an investment real estate portfolio to hold on to for future appreciation and building your net worth. Moreover, the excess financing proceeds you distribute to yourself is considered a tax-free distribution. Because you didn't sell anything, refinancing isn't considered a taxable event!

As long as people need the use of property then there will be a market demand for desirable real estate. As long as there is a market demand for desirable real estate, there will be an opportunity to "manufacture" it. You can enter the "manufacturing" business by creating value in less desirable real estate by repositioning it to be more desirable. You can make amazing profits in the process!

Welcome to this "manufacturing" business. I'm glad you're joining me!

A *ppendix*

1

SAMPLE CONDOMINIUM CONVERSION PROFIT-AND-LOSS COMPARISON SHEET

The following appendixes will help you acquire, finance, rehab, reposition, and sell commercial and investment properties. Be sure to alter the forms and calculations to fit your particular situation. Please use the forms as a general guide and have an attorney and your advisors review any legal forms before you use them in your transactions.

Determination of the Number of Units in Project Cost/Benefit 11 Units versus 8 Units

Gross Selling Price	11–Unit Project	8-Unit Project
8 one-bedrooms @ $210,000	$1,680,000	
1 two-bedrooms @ $310,000	$310,000	
1 three-bedroom duplex @ $375,000	$375,000	
1 two-bedroom garden @ $260,000	$260,000	
6 two-bedrooms @ $310,000		$1,860,000
2 two-bedroom garden @ $260,000		$520,000
5 parking spaces @ $18,000	$90,000	$90,000
Total gross sell out	*$2,715,000*	*$2,470,000*
Property cost	$1,100,000	$1,100,000

Construction cost	$1,000,000	$750,000
Gross profit	*$615,000*	*$620,000*
Carry cost (9 months, 5 percent)	$70,000	$60,000
Sales commissions (2.5 percent)	$67,875	$61,750
Miscellaneous costs	$20,000	$20,000
Total Project soft costs	*$157,875*	*$141,750*
Project Net Return on Investment	*$457,125*	*$478,250*

2

SAMPLE LETTER TO TARGETED INVESTMENT PROPERTY OWNERS TO INDUCE SELLING

Dear Investment Property Owner:

My company, as a principal, is interested in purchasing your apartment building from you.

Although we're licensed real estate brokers, we're not seeking a listing or a commission from you. Prime Property Investors, Ltd. is an experienced investment property owner with the knowledge, resources, and experience to close a transaction without delay. We're direct buyers looking to purchase your property. We make all-cash offers without cumbersome contingencies.

You'll deal directly with principals and get quick answers and maximum value without the cost of a real estate commission.

To confidentially discuss the sale of your building in an easy no-nonsense transaction, contact me directly at (847) 562-1700.

Very truly yours,
Michael H. Zaransky
CEO

P.S. It's a Seller's Market, and we're the buyer for your building!

3

SAMPLE COVER SHEET FOR A RESALE MARKETING PACKAGE FOR A REPOSITIONED APARTMENT BUILDING

Exclusive Listing

**Westmoor Apartments
Chicagoland Apartment Association
Vintage Property of the Year Award Winner
1 to 9 South View at Galena, Aurora, Illinois
$2,000,000**

One-of-a-kind 34-unit
restored vintage brick courtyard building
attention to detail, rarely a vacancy
12 two-bedroom five-room, 17 one-bedroom four-room,
& 5 large studio apartments

Located at the entry to the quaint Historic District of Aurora, Illinois, the Westmoor Apartments is a one-of-a-kind majestic building. As the winner of the Chicagoland Apartment Association Vintage Property of the Year CAMME Award, the building is an excellent example of apartment living with original vintage features and expertly detailed maintenance and upkeep. Located in an area of primarily single-family homes, quiet tree-lined streets, and some condominiums, the property provides some of the only rentals available in the neighborhood.

Convenience to the revived Downtown Aurora River District and the Aurora Metra Station makes the building location ideal and highly sought after. The property is almost always 100 percent occupied with on-location signage providing a steady stream of future rental prospects and a waiting list.

Building upgrades include all new copper horizontal water pipes, upgraded electrical service with circuit breakers, a Peerless gas steam boiler, sidewalk replacement, wrought iron fencing, landscaping, hallway painting, and exterior building and masonry chemical cleaning.

The steady income stream provides the investor with an immediate current return. There is an opportunity for further income enhancement by bringing all rents to current market levels and continuing to increase rents due to the lack of available supply of apartment rentals in the neighborhood.

Contact:
Michael H. Zaransky, CEO
Prime Property Investors, Ltd.
(847) 562-1700
Illinois Broker-Owned Property

LETTER OF INTENT FOR AN APARTMENT BUILDING OR INCOME-PRODUCING COMMERCIAL PROPERTY

LETTER OF INTENT

Via email (insert email address here) and Federal Express next-day delivery
ABC Realtors
1234 Any Street
Any Town, USA 99999
Re: Insert property address here

Dear Mr. or Ms. Realtor:

This letter of intent will evidence the intent of a to-be-formed LLC affiliated with our company, or its assignee or designee (the "Purchaser") to enter into a contract of purchase with the Owner of Record (the "Seller") for the purchase by Purchaser of the real estate property commonly known as "Insert Property Address Here" with a total of "Insert Number of Units Here" apartment units (the "Property"). The purchase by Purchaser shall be on the terms and subject to the conditions set forth below:

1. At the closing of the transaction (the Closing), Seller shall sell the property to Purchaser free and clear of all liens, encumbrances, claims or interests of any kind other than existing leases and other exceptions permitted as set forth in the legally binding, written agreement to be negotiated and entered into by Purchaser and Seller.

2. Purchase Price: In consideration of the sale and transfer of the property, Purchaser shall pay the Seller the total sum of Four Million Dollars ($4,000,000.00), adjusted for prorations, at closing, for rent, and other similar items ("Purchase Price").

3. **Earnest Money:** The purchase price shall be payable with an earnest money deposit, to be held by "Insert Name of Listing Broker Here" REALTORS®, to bear interest for the benefit of Purchaser of the sum of $100,000 due upon execution of this letter of intent and the $3,900,000 balance, plus or minus prorations, payable to Seller at closing.

4. **Commission:** Seller agrees to pay all real estate sales commission due "List Names of Any Brokers Here" in connection with the transaction. Seller and Purchaser warrant there are no other brokers entitled to compensation in connection with the transaction.

5. **Due Diligence Period:** The obligation of Purchaser to purchase the property is conditioned upon the performance by Purchaser of such inspections and due diligence as Purchaser deems appropriate or necessary including, but not limited to, appraisal, financial and lender due diligence, environmental, structural, and mechanical inspections of the land, and improvements comprising the Property. Purchaser shall complete all such inspections and due diligence on or before "Insert End of Due Diligence Date Here." Seller shall fully cooperate with Purchaser in connection with such inspections and due diligence and allow Purchaser, and Purchaser's representatives, access, upon reasonable notice,

to the property, and will provide Purchaser with any information Purchaser deems reasonably necessary or desirable in connection with such inspections and due diligence. If at any time prior to (insert end of due diligence date here), Purchaser determines in Purchaser's sole judgment that the property is unacceptable to Purchaser, for any reason or no reason, written notice shall be given to Seller, or Seller's agent stating that the property has been rejected and thereupon, this letter on intent and subsequent contract for the purchase of the property shall be deemed null and void and all monies deposited as earnest money by Purchaser shall immediately be returned to Purchaser.

6. Seller shall allow Purchaser, and Purchaser's representatives, access to the property, upon reasonable notice, at reasonable times, prior to the closing of the transaction.

7. Seller shall install a new shingle roof on the property prior to and as a condition to the closing of this transaction. In addition, Seller shall be responsible for all apartment unit make ready and turn over costs and shall make all apartments ready for occupancy in connection with the August, 2005 turnover and fall semester term occupancy. Seller shall return the 2004/2005 lease security deposits to tenants who have terminated their leases pursuant to the terms of the leases.

8. The purchase contemplated herein includes substantial personal property including, but, not limited to, partially furnished apartment units, appliances, kitchens, and other personal property. Seller shall furnish a schedule of all personal property to be included in the purchase within ten days of acceptance of this letter of intent.

9. Seller will assign all leases per the attached rent roll beginning August, 2005. As of the date of this letter of intent, all units, with the exception on units 4 and 6 (two vacant units) at the property have leases in place for the

2005/2006 school year. The vacant units 4 and 6 shall be rented for the 12-month school year at $880 per month rent each prior to closing. If at the closing the vacant units haven't been rented for the school year, Seller will pay Purchaser the sum of $10,560 for each vacant unit.

10. Purchaser and Seller agree to use their best efforts to a) enter a legally binding contract of purchase within five days, and b) close the transaction contemplated hereby on "Insert Closing Date Here."

11. The Purchaser and Seller agree that this letter of intent outlines the terms and conditions upon which Purchaser will enter a legally binding agreement to purchase the Property from Seller and that the purchase of the property is specifically conditioned upon the completion of the inspections required under number 5 above, to the satisfaction of the Purchaser. The final legally binding agreement to purchase and all sale documents must be in a form acceptable to both Purchaser and Seller and their respective legal counsel.

Very truly yours,
Michael H. Zaransky
CEO

This letter of intent is void and withdrawn if not accepted with an executed copy returned to Purchaser on or before <u>(insert deadline for acceptance date here)</u>.

Acknowledged and Agreed To:

Seller: _____

Date: _____

Required Disclosure: Michael H. Zaransky, Barbara J. Gaffen, some of their affiliates, and Prime Property Investors, Ltd. are licensed Real Estate Brokers in the State of Illinois.

5

SAMPLE RIDER TO FORM CONTRACT

Following is our company's form of a rider to a real estate contract for a typical student housing transaction. Every transaction is unique and the form will require modifications to meet the special circumstances of a particular real estate deal.

While the rider form and our typical offer complements a contract that is an all-cash offer without mortgage contingencies, the rider makes provisions for a due diligence review period, preventing the Seller from executing leases without consent prior to closing. This review period allows you access to the property prior to closing; further specification of the personal property made a part of the sale; a Seller's minimum rent guarantee; and the potential for a management agreement at a set fee with an entity related to the Seller.

RIDER TO REAL ESTATE SALES CONTRACT

This rider is attached to and made a part of that certain contract dated (insert date here), for the purchase of the real estate commonly known as (insert address here).

1. **Due Diligence Period:** The obligation of Purchaser to purchase the property is conditioned upon the performance by Purchaser of such inspections and due diligence as Purchaser deems appropriate or necessary including, but not limited to, appraisal, financial due diligence, environmental, structural, and mechanical inspections of the land and improvements comprising the Property. Purchaser shall complete all such inspections and due diligence on or before (insert date here). Seller shall fully cooperate with Purchaser in connection with such inspections and due diligence and allow Purchaser, and Purchaser's representatives, access, upon reasonable notice, to the property, and will provide Purchaser with any information Purchaser deems reasonably necessary or desirable in connection with such inspections and due diligence. If at any time prior to (insert date here), Purchaser determines in Purchaser's sole judgment that the property is unacceptable to Purchaser, for any reason or no reason, written notice shall be given to Seller, or Seller's agent, stating that the property has been rejected and thereupon, this contract shall be deemed null and void and all monies deposited as earnest money by Purchaser shall immediately be returned to Purchaser.

2. Upon acceptance of this contract, Seller shall not enter any new leases or extensions of existing leases, other than on a month to month basis, for any rental space at the property without the advance written consent of the Purchaser.

3. Seller shall allow Purchaser access to the property, upon reasonable notice, at reasonable times, prior to the closing of the transaction.

4. The purchase contemplated herein includes substantial personal property including, but, not limited to, fully fur-

nished town home properties, appliances, kitchens, and other personal property. Seller shall furnish a schedule of all personal property to be included in the purchase within ten days of acceptance of the contract.

5. Sellers will guarantee Purchaser a "minimum gross income stream" on in place leases at closing, covering the 20XX/20XX school year, effective for the twelve-month period beginning May 1, 20XX to April 30, 20XX of (enter dollar amount here). "Minimum gross income stream" shall be determined at closing by taking the aggregate of all payments due on in-place leases covering the property for the specified period. Should the aggregate of all payments due for the specified lease period calculate to an amount lower than the (enter dollar amount) minimum guarantee, Seller shall pay the difference to Purchaser at closing.

6. At Purchaser's option, Seller shall cause _____ to enter into a management agreement (Manager-Owner Agreement) covering the property, upon terms and conditions acceptable to _____ and Purchaser with a management fee equal to 8% of gross monthly rental income.

Required Disclosure: Barbara J Gaffen and Michael H. Zaransky, principals of Purchaser and Prime Property Investors, Ltd., are licensed Real Estate Brokers in the State of Illinois.

(Date)
Purchaser:Seller:

_____

Prime Property Acquisitions, LLC,
As nominee for an Illinois Limited
Liability Company to be formed,
Michael H. Zaransky, Member

6

DUE DILIGENCE CHECKLIST FOR STUDENT HOUSING

Property Specific Review and Confirmation

Data furnished by Sellers independently verified or tested:

1. _____ Full accountant's reports of income and expenses for past three years plus current year to date

2. _____ Copies of all leases for the new academic term

3. _____ Copies of last year's real estate and personal property tax bills

4. _____ Copies of all utility and scavenger bills for current and last three years

5. _____ Copies of paid repair and maintenance bills for current and last three years

6. _____ Rental payment delinquency reports

7. _____ Current rent roll

8. _____ Schedule of security deposits

9. _____ Schedule of advance rent payments (last month's rent and other)

10. _____ Copies of all invoices and contracts for major building improvements including recent new roof

11. _____ Copies of all environmental, engineering, and appraisal reports

12. _____ List of names and phone numbers of all vendors

13. _____ Copies of any property plans, blueprints, and room layouts for buildings

14. _____ Copies of any existing management agreement and any written service contracts or warranties still in effect

15. _____ Plat of survey

16. _____ Copies of any correspondence or filings relating to any resident disputes, controversies, or litigation

Data and inspection performed or verified by third parties or buyer:

1. _____ Complete inspection of all apartments and common areas

2. _____ Mechanical systems inspection

3. _____ Roof and structure inspection

4. _____ City code compliance and certificate of occupancy

5. _____ Inspection of property grounds and parking lot

6. _____ Compile data on lease-up dates and rental rates for new academic term leases

Market-specific due diligence:

1. _____ Review local city or village master plan

2. _____ Interview potential local third-party management companies

   - _____ Opinion of local housing market
   - _____ Opinion of subject property
   - _____ Opinion as to ability to increase rents
   - _____ Budget for operation of property
   - _____ Quote for management of property

Order written third-party reports:

1. _____ Phase I environmental
2. _____ Engineering
3. _____ Roof consultant
4. _____ Appraisal
5. _____ Survey
6. _____ Title

SAMPLE LETTER FROM DEVELOPER TO TURN OVER MANAGEMENT TO A CONDOMINIUM ASSOCIATION

To: Condominium Unit Owners
123 Main Street   Chicago
Re: Condominium Association Meeting

Turnover of Records and Operations to Unit Owners

I've been in touch with Sam who has agreed to host all of you at his condominium (unit 15-B) for the organizational meeting of the Condominium Association. The meeting will take place at Sam's condominium unit on Monday, August 30th at 7:00 P.M. You can reach Sam around the building or via email at *SamTheCondoResident@server.com.*

In order to effectuate a smooth meeting for everyone, I've enclosed several items for each of you in connection with your commencing the operation and management of the Association by the unit owners. Among the items enclosed is a copy of the resignation of all the internal developer officers and directors of the Association. You'll be required to replace the resigned positions with your own memberships. Illinois Condominium Associations require a minimum of three directors, a president, and a secretary.

I am pleased to be able to turn over to the Association such a great building in very sound financial shape. After the pay-in of all assessments due to date from the unit owners, you'll end up with a bank balance in excess of $30,000, with insurance fully paid for the initial year. Given the initial operating budget of $50,560 (including the full insurance premium) per year, you have a substantial financial cushion as you commence operations.

Although I've enclosed detailed schedules as well as a copy of the filed Declaration of Condominium for each of your records, I've furnished Sam with a package that includes backup materials including copies of each paid invoice and the recorded condominium Plat of Survey. I've also provided Sam with a check for the full balance in the current Condominium Association account, made payable to the Association, so you can select a bank convenient for your needs for the deposit of all Association funds.

Enclosed for your records and use in connection with the operation of the Association are the following:

1. Copy of the estimated operating budget for the Association
2. Copy of the resignations of the current Association officers and directors
3. Schedule of initial budgeted monthly assessments by unit and month of closing
4. Initial invoice to each unit owner and developer for assessments due the Association
5. Bank account reconciliation with copies of all checks deposited, copy of two checks written, and monthly bank statements
6. Schedule of reimbursement of Association expenses due to the developer paid by us on behalf of the Association

7. Internal Revenue Service SS-4 Form registering the Association and receiving a federal identification number for the Association

8. Filed copy of the Articles of Incorporation under the Not-For-Profit Corporation Act with the Illinois Secretary of State

9. Landscaping contract that you have the option to cancel

10. Warranty covering the new and repaired exterior system in the rear portion of the building

11. Copy of the Recorded Condominium Declaration and By-Laws of the Association

In addition, I have furnished Sam with originals of the following items:

1. Check made payable to the Association for the current net bank balance

2. Paid invoices for amounts reimbursable to the developer paid on behalf of the Association

3. *A Guide for Organizing Not-For-Profit Corporations* issued by the Illinois Secretary of State

4. An additional copy of the condominium Plat of Survey

5. Condominium Association insurance policies

We hope you continue to enjoy your condominiums. Best of luck to you all as you take over the operations of the Association. Should you have any questions, feel free to contact me via email and I will try to help.

8

SAMPLE NET PROFIT PROJECTION FOR A CONDOMINIUM CONVERSION REHAB AND REPOSITIONING PROJECT

Prime Property Investors, Ltd.
12234 Main Street Chicago
44 Unit Condominium Conversion Project
Projected Return: Fall Winter 2005

Gross condominium selling price	
2 one-bedroom (Garden) @ $140,000	$280,000
16 one-bedroom (3 Room) @ $175,000	$2,800,000
26 one-bedroom (4 Room) @ $185,000	$4,810,000
Total selling price	*$7,890,000*
Expense of project	
Property cost	$5,000,000
Renovation construction $15,000 per unit × 44	$660,000
Common area/exterior	$250,000
GC fee	$100,000
Total property and renovation cost	*($6,010,000)*
Gross profit	**$1,880,000**

Interest expense (80% / 7%, 6 months)	$160,000
Sales commission (5%)	$394,500
Miscellaneous other cost	$88,000
Total project soft cost	*($642,500)*
Projected net profit on project (15.6% of sellout)	*$1,237,500*
Increase return with $10,000 per unit renovation cost	*$220,000*
Revised net profit on project (18.5% of sellout)	*$1,457,500*
Equity	$1,202,000
Debt	$4,808,000

9

SAMPLE CONDOMINIUM CONVERSION UNIT PURCHASE AGREEMENT

CONDOMINIUM PURCHASE AGREEMENT

1. **Parties.** The following are the parties to this 12234 Main Street Purchase Agreement

   a) **Name of Purchaser:** _____

      and _____

      Home Address:_____

      _____

      Phone: _____

      Email: _____

      Fax: _____

      Business Address: _____

      _____

      Phone: _____

   b) **Seller:** ABC Management, Inc., an Illinois corporation company whose address is c/o Prime Property Investors, 1234 Any Street, Any Town, Illinois 99999.

2. **Purchase of Condominium Unit.** Seller agrees to sell, and Purchaser agrees to purchase, for the Purchase Price

(hereinafter defined), subject to the terms and conditions of the Declaration (hereinafter defined), and upon the terms and conditions hereinafter set forth, (a) Residential Unit No._____ (the "Residential Unit") at 12234 Main Street, Chicago, Illinois (as defined in the Declaration) (the "Building"), (b) Parking Unit No_____ as shown in the Declaration ([together] the "Parking Unit") (the Residential Unit and the Parking Unit being sometimes collectively referred to herein as the "Purchased Unit"), and (c) an undivided _____ percent interest, subject to change in accordance with the provisions of the Declaration, in the "Common Elements" of the real estate legally described on Exhibit A of the Declaration, as amended from time to time. The Purchased Unit and its corresponding percentage interest in the Common Elements are herein collectively called the "Unit Ownership." The real estate submitted to the Act, as defined below, from time to time pursuant to the Declaration, and the improvements to be constructed thereon, are herein collectively called the "Property."

3. **Construction.** Seller anticipates that the Purchased Unit and the Building shall be substantially completed on or about January 15, 2004 (the "Anticipated Date"), and agrees to use reasonable efforts to substantially complete the Purchased Unit and Building on or before said date in substantial compliance with the outline plans and outline specifications therefor (the "Plans") prepared by Architect & Associates (the "Architect"), which Plans are available for Purchaser's inspection during business hours at the sales office of Seller, and which Plans are, by this reference, deemed a part hereof. In the event Seller does not substantially complete construction of the Purchased Unit and the Building by March 1, 2004, after the Anticipated Date (as such date may be extended pursuant to the terms

hereof), Purchaser shall have the right to terminate this Agreement by giving written notice thereof to Seller prior to the time Seller substantially completes the Purchased Unit and the Building, in which case the Purchaser shall receive a refund of all Earnest Money and other payments made by Purchaser to Seller pursuant to the terms of this Agreement, and the parties hereto shall have no further rights or obligations under this Agreement (other than the obligations of Purchaser under Paragraph 15 of this Agreement). Seller shall not be responsible for delays in the construction of the Purchased Unit or the Building resulting from acts of God, strikes, wars, riots, governmental regulation or restriction, material or labor shortage, the unavailability of mortgage financing, or other cause, casualty, or circumstance beyond the reasonable control of Seller, or any other event which would support a defense based upon impossibility of performance for reasons beyond Seller's control, and in the event of such delay, Seller shall be allowed such additional time as may be caused by such delay to substantially complete this work.

4. **Purchase Price and Other Payments.**

   a) The Purchase Price for the Unit Ownership shall be as follows:

   Purchase Price for the Residential Unit: $ ____ ____

   Upgrade selection price for Residential Unit: $__ __

   Purchase Price for the Parking Unit: + $___ _____

   Total Purchase Price for the Unit Ownership

   (the "Purchase Price"): $_____

   The Purchase Price shall be payable as follows:

   Initial payment of Earnest Money in an amount equal to $2,500 shall be deposited with Seller simultaneously with Purchaser's execution hereof: $_____

   Additional Earnest Money in an amount such that the deposit equals 10 percent of the Purchase Price

shall be due and payable within five business days of
Seller's acceptance of this agreement: $ _____
The balance of the Purchase Price shall be paid at the
Closing (hereinafter defined): $ _____

_____   _____

    Seller's Initials   Purchaser's Initials

b) Any deposit, payment, or advance in the payment
    of the Purchase Price received by Seller for the Unit
    Ownership pursuant to subsections (i) or (ii) of sub-
    paragraph 4(b) above, other than a payment made
    for Extras (hereinafter defined), shall be deemed to
    be "Earnest Money" and shall be held in an interest-
    bearing escrow account, with interest thereon payable
    to Purchaser.

c) The balance of the Purchase Price, plus or minus
    applicable prorations, together with closing costs,
    lender's charges, tax deposits, if any, and contribu-
    tions by Purchaser to the working capital and reserves
    of the 12234 Main Street Condominium Association
    (the "Association"), as provided in Paragraph 4(e)
    below, is due and payable at the Closing. The Pur-
    chase Price shall be paid in cash, certified check, or
    a bank cashier's check. Time is of the essence with
    respect to Purchaser's payment obligations under this
    Paragraph 4.

d) At Closing, the Purchaser shall also pay to the Asso-
    ciation an amount equal to three months' assessment
    of purchaser's pro rata share of Common Expenses
    (as defined in the Declaration), determined in
    accordance with the Declaration. Such amount shall
    represent Purchaser's pro rata share of the initial
    reserve capital fund as provided in the Declaration.
    Seller shall require such assessment to be similarly

paid by every purchaser of a Unit (as defined in the Declaration).

e) In the event that Seller is unable to collect, upon presentment, any check delivered by Purchaser in payment of the Earnest Money, then, at Seller's option, this Agreement shall become null and void and of no further force or effect, in which case all payments received by Seller pursuant to the terms of this Agreement shall be retained by Seller, and the parties hereto shall have no further rights or obligations under this Agreement [other than the obligations of Purchaser under Paragraphs 12(a) and 15 of this Agreement].

5. **Condominium Documents.**

a) Prior to the Closing, Seller shall cause to be recorded, in the office of the Recorder of Deeds of Cook County, Illinois, in accordance with the Illinois Condominium Property Act (the "Act") and the Municipal Code of Chicago (the "Code"), the following documents:

   i) The Declaration of Condominium for 12234 Main Street Condominium Association (the "Declaration"); and

   ii) The Plat (the "Plat") filed with the Declaration, as provided in the Act, showing the Building and the Purchased Unit.

b) After the recordation of the Plat, a copy of the Plat shall be available for inspection by Purchaser at the office of Seller during reasonable business hours.

c) Prior to the Purchaser's execution of this Agreement, a copy of each of the following documents was delivered to Purchaser: (i) the floor plan of the Purchased Unit (a copy of which floor plan is attached hereto as Exhibit B); (ii) the Declaration; (iii) the By-Laws of the Association (the "By-Laws"); and (iv) the estimated operating budget and estimated monthly assessments of the Association. Said delivered documents are herein collectively referred to as the "Condominium Documents."

d) PURCHASER HEREBY ACKNOWLEDGES RECEIPT OF THE CONDOMINIUM DOCUMENTS AND OF HIS OR HER OPPORTUNITY TO REVIEW SUCH CONDOMINIUM DOCUMENTS. PURCHASER ACKNOWLEDGES THAT UPON CLOSING HE OR SHE WILL BECOME A MEMBER OF THE ASSOCIA-TION, AND AGREES THAT, FROM AND AFTER CLOSING, HE OR SHE SHALL BE BOUND BY AND COMPLY WITH THE PROVISIONS OF, AND PERFORM ALL THE OBLIGATIONS IMPOSED ON UNIT OWNERS BY, THE ACT, THE DECLARA-TION, AND THE BY-LAWS.

e) Seller reserves the right to make any changes in the Condominium Documents permitted by law, subject to the provisions of Section 22 of the Act. To the extent that Section 22 of the Act requires Purchaser's approval of certain changes in the condominium Documents, Purchaser's sole remedy in the event of Purchaser's nonapproval of such change shall be to rescind this Agreement within the time and in the manner provided in the Act. Purchaser acknowledges that minor changes and adjustment in the floor plan and dimensions of the Purchased Unit deemed by Seller necessary to accommodate structural and mechanical requirements, changes in the percentage of ownership, if any, pursuant to the Declaration, and changes in the Condominium Documents in order to enable Unit Purchasers to qualify for loans to be made, insured, guaranteed, or purchased by any governmental authority or any quasi-governmental authority shall not be considered material changes in the Condominium Documents requiring Purchaser's approval under Section 22 of the Act.

6. **Conveyance of Title.** At the Closing, Seller shall cause title to the Unit Ownership to be conveyed to Purchaser by a recordable, special warranty deed subject only to the following exceptions (the "Permitted Exceptions"): (a) general real estate taxes for the previous and current year not then due and for subsequent years, including taxes which may accrue by reason of new or additional improvements during the year of Closing; (b) special taxes or assessments for improvements not yet completed; (c) easements, covenants, restrictions, agreements, conditions, and building lines of record and party wall rights; (d) the Act; (e) the Plat; (f) terms, provisions, and conditions of the Condominium Documents, including all amendments and exhibits thereto; (g) applicable zoning and building laws and ordinances; (h) the Code; (i) unrecorded public and quasi-public utility easements, if any; (j) Purchaser's mortgage, if any; (k) plats of dedication and plats of subdivision and covenants thereon; (l) leases, licenses, operating agreements, and other agreements affecting the Common Elements; (m) acts done or suffered by or judgments against Purchaser, or anyone claiming under Purchaser; (n) liens and other matters of title over which the Title Company (as hereinafter defined) is willing to insure without cost to Purchaser, (o) encroachments, if any; and (p) the rights to cable television and T-1 providers. If Purchaser is a husband and wife, their interest hereunder shall be as joint tenants, and not as tenants in common or tenants by the entirety, and title shall be conveyed accordingly unless Purchaser shall direct Seller, in writing, to the contrary not less than 30 days prior to Closing.

7. **Extras**. Purchaser shall have the opportunity to negotiate an agreement with Seller, on a form provided by Seller, for certain upgrades, additions, deletions, changes, or modifications (together "Extras") (as determined by Seller). In the event that Purchaser and Seller shall execute an order (an "Extra Order") for Extras, said Extra Order will not in any way alter, affect, or otherwise impact the Plans or delay the completion of the Purchased Unit. No Extra will be made or installed by Seller unless both parties hereto shall have agreed to such Extra and the price therefor in an Extra Order. No broker, employee, subcontractor, sales agent, or representative of Seller has authority to agree to or comply with a verbal request by Purchaser for any Extra. Notwithstanding anything herein contained to the contrary, Seller shall have no obligation to agree to any Extra.

8. **Changes: Add-Ons**. Seller reserves the right, without notice to Purchaser, to make any reasonable changes deemed necessary in the Purchased Unit and/or Common Elements, including room sizes for structural or mechanical reasons, but no changes shall be made which affect the physical location or the basic design of the Purchased Unit. In the event of the inability of the Seller to obtain certain materials required by the Plans, Seller shall have the right, without notice to Purchaser, to substitute other material or brand names of similar or better quality, utility, or color. Seller reserves the right, without notice to Purchaser, to make any changes in construction as may be required by material or labor shortages, strikes, acts of God, war, stoppages, or such other emergency situations or other causes beyond Seller's control, including, without limitation, changes in or enactment of any applicable federal, state, or local laws, ordinances, regulations, or statues.

9. **Limited Warranty.** Upon Closing, Seller shall extend to Purchaser the warranties covering the Purchased Unit in accordance with the terms and provisions set forth on Exhibit C attached hereto and made a part hereof. THE EXPRESS LIMITED WARRANTIES CONTAINED IN THIS AGREEMENT, SPECIFICALLY INCLUDING EXHIBIT C ATTACHED HERETO AND MADE A PART HEREOF, ARE THE ONLY WARRANTIES MADE BY SELLER IN CONNECTION WITH ITS CONSTRUCTION AND SALE OF THE PURCHASED UNIT, AND SUCH WARRANTIES ARE MADE IN PLACE OF ALL OTHER WARRANTIES, WHETHER ARISING FROM CUSTOM, USAGE, COURSE OR TRADE, STATUTORY OR CASE LAW, OR OTHERWISE. SELLER MAKES NO WARRANTY WHICH IS NOT SET OUT OR SPECIFICALLY REFERENCED IN THIS AGREEMENT, AND SELLER AND PURCHASER ACKNOWLEDGE, UNDERSTAND, AND AGREE THAT ANY AND ALL IMPLIED WARRANTIES AS TO THE QUALITY OR CONDITION OF THE PURCHASED UNIT ARE HEREBY DISCLAIMED AND WAIVED, INCLUDING ANY IMPLIED WARRANTY OF HABITABILITY OR THAT THE PURCHASED UNIT WILL BE REASONABLY SUITED FOR ITS INTENDED USE, FREE OF LATENT DEFECTS, AS WELL AS WARRANTIES OF MERCHANTABILITY AND FITNESS FOR A PARTICULAR PURPOSE RELATING TO WARRANTED ITEMS, CONDITIONS, OR PROCESS WHICH DO NOT CONSTITUTE "CONSUMER PRODUCTS" UNDER PUBLIC LAW 920637, COMMONLY KNOWN AS THE MAGNUSSON-MOSS ACT.

10. **Personal Property.** Seller shall deliver to Purchaser a bill of sale for all personal property listed on Exhibit A attached hereto and made a part hereof. Seller shall deliver to Purchaser at Closing all manufacturers' warranties, if any, covering consumer products to be conveyed to Pur-

chaser hereunder, provided, however, that Seller shall not thereby be deemed to warrant any such consumer products in any way, either expressed or implied, or to adopt any such manufacture's warranty thereof. AS TO SUCH PERSONAL PROPERTY AND AS TO ANY CONSUMER PRODUCT (AS THAT TERM MAY BE DEFINED UNDER APPLICABLE FEDERAL, STATE, OR LOCAL LAWS) WHICH MAY BE CONTAINED IN THE PURCHASED UNIT, AND AS TO THE COMMON ELEMENTS SELLER NEITHER MAKES NOR ADOPTS ANY WARRANTY WHATSOEVER, AND SPECIFICALLY EXCLUDES AND DISCLAIMS EXPRESS OR IMPLIED WARRANTIES OF ANY NATURE INCLUDING ANY IMPLIED WARRANTY OF MERCHANTABILITY, SUITABILITY, OR FITNESS FOR A PARTICULAR PURPOSE. Seller shall not be responsible for the implementation of any corrective work that is included in any manufacturer's or supplier's warranty received by Seller in connection with any personal property or consumer product in the Purchased Unit and delivered to Purchaser.

11. **<u>Closing</u>.**

   a) The closing (the "Closing") of the sale and purchase contemplated herein shall be on a date (the "Closing Date") selected by Seller. If construction of the Purchased Unit and the Building has been completed on the date this Agreement is executed by Purchaser, the Closing Date shall be _____ _____. Seller shall not be responsible for delays in the construction of the Purchased Unit or the building resulting from acts of God, strikes, wars, riots, governmental regulation or restriction, material or labor shortage, the unavailability or mortgage financing, or other cause or circumstance beyond the reasonable control of Seller, or any other event which would support a defense based upon impossibility of performance for reasons beyond Seller's control, and in the event of such delay, Seller shall be allowed such additional time as may be caused by such delay to substantially complete such construction. Seller's failure to complete the landscaping, walks, driveways, and any other outside work in connection with the Unit Ownership prior to the Closing shall, under no circumstances, delay the Closing or excuse Purchaser from meeting all obligations required of him or her hereunder, except that Seller's obligations to complete such landscaping, walks, driveways, and any other work shall continue after the Closing. There shall be no "hold-backs" or other credits against or reduction of the Purchase Price for the Unit Ownership as a result of any such incomplete items. Purchaser shall complete all closing papers and mortgage papers in preparation for the Closing when requested to do so by the Seller or the mortgage lender.

b) Closing shall take place at the office of Attorneys' Title Guaranty Fund, 321 Elm Street, Normal, Illinois or any other title company currently doing business in the Chicago, Illinois metropolitan area as may be selected by Seller (the "Title Company"). The Closing shall be on an agency basis, provided that, at Seller's option, the Closing shall occur pursuant to the terms of a deed and money escrow agreement then furnished and in use by the Title Company, as amended to conform with this Agreement, the cost of which escrow agreement shall be paid equally by Purchaser and Seller.

c) Any fee charged by the Title Company for the agency closing or any moneylender's escrow establish with the Title Company by Purchaser or his or her mortgage lender, if any, shall be paid by Purchaser. Seller shall pay the title charges customarily charged to sellers by the Title Company, including any state or county related estate transfer tax, and the Purchaser shall pay any such charges customarily charged to purchasers, including the charge for recording Purchaser's deed and the charge for continuation of the title search to cover such recording. Purchaser shall also pay any local or municipal real estate transfer tax imposed by the City of Chicago.

d) Seller shall not be liable for any inconvenience, loss, or damage suffered by Purchaser resulting from any delay in Closing, however caused.

e) At or prior to Closing, Seller shall furnish Purchaser a survey of the Property indicating the location of the Purchased Unit. At the Closing, the Title Company or its title policy issuing affiliate shall be prepared to issue to Purchaser, at Seller's expense, an ALTA owner's title insurance policy (the "Title Policy"), in the amount of the Purchase Price, showing title to the Unit Ownership in Purchaser subject only to the following: (i) the Permitted Exceptions; (ii) the usual title exceptions contained in owner's title insurance policies issued by the Title Company or its title policy-issuing affiliate, with an extended coverage endorsement insuring over general exceptions; and (iii) such prohibited exceptions as to which the Title Company or its title policy issuing affiliate shall be prepared to issue an endorsement in the usual and customary form provided by the Title Company or its title policy-issuing affiliate to the Title Policy, insuring Purchaser against any loss or damage which Purchaser may suffer or incur by reason of such unpermitted exceptions. The Title Commitment shall be conclusive evidence of good title.

f) At Closing, Purchaser shall deposit Purchaser's pro rata share of the initial reserve capital fund [as provided in subparagraph 4(e) above] and the balance of the Purchase Price, plus or minus applicable prorations, charges, or costs as specified in the closing statement delivered to Purchaser, and the documents required by Purchaser's mortgage lender, if any; and Purchaser shall cause Purchaser's mortgage lender, if any, to deposit the proceeds of Purchaser's mortgage loan. At Closing, an amount equal to Purchaser's pro rata share of the initial reserve capital fund shall be paid by the Title Company to the Association for the account of Purchaser. Seller may use the sale proceeds payable to Seller at the Closing to release any lien securing any land and/or construction loan relating to the Unit Ownership or any mechanic's lien or materialman's lien relating to the Unit Ownership.

g) Intentionally Omitted

h) Insurance premiums advanced by Seller for the permanent insurance on the Unit Ownership, monthly assessments on the Unit Ownership, and other usual and customary proration items (other than general real estate taxes) shall be adjusted ratably as of the Closing.

i) Real estate taxes shall be prorated based upon the most recent real estate tax assessment issued for the property, the most recent available real estate tax rate and multiplier for the property, and Purchaser's percentage ownership of the property.

12. **Possession and Occupancy.**

a) Purchaser shall be entitled to occupancy and possession of the Purchased Unit from and after the Closing and payment in full by Purchaser to Seller of the Purchase Price and all other required payments.

During construction and prior to the Closing, Seller shall have sole control and exclusive possession of the Purchased Unit. Prior to Closing, Purchaser shall not authorize or direct that any work be performed in the Purchased Unit without Seller's prior written consent. Except as expressly provided in the following subparagraph 12(b), Purchaser shall have no right to possess, occupy, or enter the Purchased Unit prior to Closing. In the event Purchaser, or person(s) or companies directed, authorized, or permitted by Purchaser to do so, enter the Purchased Unit, then Purchaser shall save, defend, indemnify, and hold harmless Seller from any and all costs, expenses and liabilities arising or claimed to arise from said entry. It is expressly agreed that the Purchaser's obligations under this subparagraph 12(a) shall survive the Closing or the earlier termination of this Agreement.

i) Purchaser shall have the right to make one inspection of the Residential Unit with Seller or Seller's representative on or about 30 days prior to the Closing at such time as shall be reasonable mutually acceptable to Seller and Purchaser. Such inspection shall be solely for the purpose of permitting Purchaser to view the Residential Unit. Purchaser shall not be entitled to submit any punch list of incomplete or incorrect work in connection with such inspection.

ii) Within 48 hours prior to the Closing, Purchaser shall make n inspection of the Purchased Unit with Seller or Seller's representative, and shall execute Seller's form of inspection report ("Inspection Report") listing all items of work that the parties mutually agree are incomplete or require correction ("Punch List Items"). If Purchaser does not appear for such inspection at the time designated by Seller in written notice to Purchaser, then Seller or Seller's representative may, but shall not be obligated to, prepare the Inspection Report on behalf of Seller and Purchaser, and the Inspection Report shall be binding on Purchaser. Seller shall complete or correct the Punch List Items prior to, or within a reasonable time after, the Closing, subject to the availability of labor or materials and other circumstances beyond the reasonable control of Seller. Purchaser will grant Seller and Seller's agents access to the Purchased Unit at reasonable times during normal business hours after Closing to complete or correct Punch List Items. Purchaser's refusal to close under this Agreement because of Purchaser's failure to make inspections prior to Closing, or Purchaser's refusal to close under this Agreement because of Seller's failure to complete all Punch List Items on the Inspection Report prior to Closing, shall constitute a default by Purchaser hereunder. Should the parties not reach agreement on Punch List Items, then disputed items shall be submitted to the Architect for determination based upon applicable customary standards or tolerances. Such determination shall be binding upon the parties.

13. **Seller's Easement.** For the purpose of completing the development, construction, marketing, and sale of all stages of the project containing the Property, Seller and Seller's successors and assigns, and Seller's agents, contractors, employees, and subcontractors are hereby given the right of ingress and egress, and other use of the Property (other than the Purchased Unit after the Closing) related to said development, construction, marketing, and sale, and are specifically given full right and authority to

maintain on the Property (other than the Purchased Unit after the Closing) signs, transient parking, sales and leasing offices, condominium association offices, model units, and administrative offices. This paragraph shall survive Closing and recording of a deed to the Unit Ownership.

14. **Assignment; Recordation.**

   a) Purchaser may not assign, set over, or transfer this Agreement or any of Purchaser's rights or interests under this Agreement, without Seller's prior written approval. Any such purported assignment by Purchaser without said approval by Seller shall be void and of no effect.

   b) Purchaser shall not record this Agreement or any memorandum hereof. If Purchaser shall record the same, then this Agreement shall, at Seller's option, become null and void, all the rights of the Purchaser hereunder shall thereupon cease and terminate and all sums (including the Earnest Money and any payments for Extras) paid to Seller shall be forfeited by Purchaser and become the sole property of Seller; provided, however, that the obligations of Purchaser under Paragraphs 12(a) and 15 of this Agreement shall survive.

15. **Broker.** Purchaser hereby represents and warrants that, other than Prime Property Investors, Ltd. (Broker") [and _____ ("Broker")], no agent or broker was instrumental in submitting, showing, or selling the Unit Ownership to Purchaser. Purchaser agrees to indemnify, defend, and hold harmless Seller and Seller's successors and assigns from and against any and all claims, damages, demands, causes of action, judgments, orders, decrees, losses, costs, expenses (including consultants' and attorneys' fees and expenses), forfeitures, charges, liabilities, initial amounts paid in settlement, fines, penal-

ties and other sanctions, of any nature whatsoever, which Seller or Seller's successors or assigns may suffer or incur by reason, of, or in connection with, all with whom Purchaser has dealt in connection with Purchaser's purchase of the Unit Ownership. It is expressly agreed that the Purchaser's obligations under this Paragraph 15 shall survive the Closing or the earlier termination of this Agreement.

16. **Notices.** All notices and demands herein required or given hereunder shall be in writing and shall be deemed sufficient if personally delivered or delivered by commercial messenger service, private express delivery, by facsimile copy with subsequent first-class mailing of original, or mailed by registered or certified mail, postage, prepaid, return receipt requested, to ABC Seller, c/o Prime Property Investors, Ltd., 1234 Any Street, Suite 506, Any Town, Illinois 99999 with a copy to Attorney at Law & Associates; 321 Maple Street; Any Town, Illinois 99999, or to Purchaser at the home or office address set forth on Page 1 of this Agreement. The date of such personal delivery, facsimile transmission, or mailing shall be deemed the date of notice.

17. Intentionally Omitted

18. **Defaults.**

   a) *Purchaser's Default.* Upon a default by Purchaser in the performance of any of Purchaser's obligations under this Agreement, Seller, at Seller's option, may terminate this Agreement, in which case all sums therefore paid to Seller by Purchaser, including but not limited to the Earnest Money, and all payments for Extras, if any, and all payments for changes set forth in Selection Change Orders, of any executed by Seller and Purchaser, and all Selection Change Order fees, shall be forfeited to Seller as liquidated damages, and the parties hereto shall have no further rights or obligations under this Agreement [other than the obligations of Purchaser under Paragraphs 12(a) and 15 of this Agreement]. A failure by Purchaser to close pursuant to the terms of this Agreement shall be a default by Purchaser under this Agreement.

b) *Seller's Default.* If Seller shall materially default in any of Seller's obligations under this Agreement, and if Purchaser shall have fully performed all of Purchaser's obligations under this Agreement, then, in addition to any other remedies that Purchaser may have at law or in equity, Purchaser may elect to (i) terminate the Agreement, in which case Purchaser shall receive a refund of all Earnest Money and other payments made by Purchaser to Seller pursuant to the terms of this Agreement, with interest, whereupon the parties hereto shall have no further rights or obligations under this Agreement [other than the obligations of Purchaser under Paragraphs 12(a) and 15 of this Agreement], or (ii) waive such defaults and to consummate the transaction contemplated by the Agreement in the same manner as if there had been no default, without any reduction in the Purchase Price and without any further claim against Seller therefor.

19. **Material Destruction.** If, prior to Closing, the Purchased Unit or a material portion of the Building, which portion is required to reasonably access the Purchased Unit, shall be destroyed or materially damaged by fire or other casualty, Seller shall have the option to repair and restore the Purchased Unit or the damaged portion of said Building to its former condition within 360 days after such damage occurs (and Closing shall be postponed accordingly) or to terminate this Agreement. In the event of such termination, all sums therefore paid to Seller shall be refunded to Purchaser, and, except for the obligations of Purchaser

under Paragraphs 12(a) and 15 of this Agreement, neither party shall have any further liability to the other.

20. **Time for Acceptance**. This Agreement, when executed by Purchaser and delivered to Seller, together with the initial payment of earnest money specified hereunder, shall constitute, for a period of seven days after the date hereof, an irrevocable offer by Purchaser to purchase the Unit Ownership. In the event Seller, by a duty authorized officer, executes this Agreement and delivers a copy thereof to Purchaser within said seven-day period, Purchaser's offer shall be deemed accepted and the Agreement binding. In the event Purchaser's offer is not so accepted within said seven-day period, all deposits made by Purchaser to Seller to date shall be returned to Purchaser and Purchaser's offer shall be deemed withdrawn.

21. **Gender**. Wherever appropriate, as used herein, the singular shall denote the plural, and the masculine, feminine, and neuter are interchangeable.

22. Intentionally Omitted

23. **Financing**.

    a) This Agreement is contingent upon the ability of Purchaser to obtain, within a period of 30 days after the date of Seller's acceptance hereof (the "Financing Period"), a mortgage commitment for $_____ or such lesser sum as Purchaser shall accept. Purchaser shall pay all charges imposed by the lender, including, but not limited to, credit, appraisal, and origination fees. Purchaser shall make diligent and accurate applications or applications of such mortgage commitment within three business days after Seller's acceptance of this Agreement, and shall immediately thereafter notify Seller of the name and address of the lender(s) at which such application was made. Purchaser shall make every reasonable effort to obtain such commitment. The parties acknowledge that it is the practice of lenders to vary interest rates, service charges, and other terms as market conditions change. Therefore, the mortgage commitment, whether obtained by Purchaser, or by Seller on behalf of Purchaser pursuant to subparagraph 23(b) below, shall be deemed obtained if a lender commits to lend Purchaser the amount stipulated above at the same interest rate, service charges, and other terms then being offered by that lender to comparable borrowers for comparable montages, it being understood that such interest rate and other charges may be subject to change pursuant to the terms of the commitment. Notwithstanding anything to the contrary, a written commitment issued by a lender is evidence of mortgage approval. If Purchaser obtains (or Seller obtains for Purchaser) the mortgage commitment contemplated above, then Purchaser shall promptly provide Seller with a copy of any such commitment, and shall be responsible for taking all actions necessary, and shall bear all costs, in order to keep said commitment in full force and effect until the Closing. Any condition set forth in the commitment, other than the completion of the construction of the Purchased Unit and the Building, is the sole responsibility of Purchaser.

b) If Purchaser is unable to obtain the above-described commitment, Purchaser shall so notify Seller thereof in writing during the Financing Period. IF SELLER IS NOT SO NOTIFIED PRIOR TO THE END OF THE FINANCING PERIOD, IT SHALL BE CONCLUSIVELY PRESUMED THAT PURCHASER HAS OBTAINED SUCH COMMITMENT OR WILL PURCHASE THE UNIT OWNERSHIP WITHOUT

MORTGAGE FINANCING. If Seller is so notified in writing prior to the end of the Financing Period, Seller may, at Seller's option, within 30 days after receipt by Seller of such notice, attempt to obtain said commitment on behalf of Purchaser. Purchaser agrees to furnish Seller and/or any potential lenders all requested credit information, and to sign customary papers relating to the application for obtaining said commitment. If Purchaser notifies Seller during the Financing Period that Purchaser was unable to obtain a mortgage commitment as aforesaid, and Seller is unable or unwilling to attempt to obtain such commitment on behalf of Purchaser as above provided, this Agreement shall be null and void, and the parties hereto shall have no further rights or obligations under this Agreement [other than the obligations of Purchaser under Paragraphs 12(a) and 15 of this Agreement], and the Earnest Money shall be returned to Purchaser.

c) Purchaser hereby grants Seller permission to review Purchaser's application for a mortgage on the Purchased Unit and the credit report obtained by any lender. By signing and submitting this instrument to Seller, Purchaser hereby authorizes Seller to secure a credit report of Purchaser. Nothing contained herein shall be deemed to constitute an undertaking by Seller to obtain or arrange for a mortgage commitment on Purchaser's behalf. Any actions which Seller may take hereunder in connection with attempting to obtain or obtaining a mortgage commitment for Purchaser shall solely as an accommodation to Purchaser, and Seller shall not be deemed an agent for Purchaser or any lender.

d) The provisions of this Paragraph 23 shall only apply if Purchaser is purchasing the Residential Unit for his or her own personal residence, to be occupied by Purchaser upon Closing.

e) In the event that Purchaser waives the requirement under subparagraph 23(a) of this Agreement that, as a condition to closing, Purchaser be able to obtain a mortgage commitment, or in the event Purchaser shall not notify Seller in writing during the Financing Period that Purchaser has been unable to obtain a financing commitment, then Purchaser shall promptly provide to Seller financial statements, tax returns, and other documents as shall be reasonably required by Seller to confirm the ability of Purchaser to close the purchase of the Purchased Unit without mortgage financing. If, after receiving and reviewing such documents, Seller, in Seller's sole and absolute discretion, believes that Purchaser will not be able to close the purchase of the Purchased Unit without mortgage financing, then Seller, at Seller's option, may terminate this Agreement, whereupon this Agreement shall be null and void, and the parties to the Agreement shall have no future rights or obligations under the Agreement [other than the obligations of Purchaser under Paragraph 12(a) and 15 of the Agreement], and the Earnest Money shall be returned to Purchaser.

24. **Binding Agreement.** This Agreement shall be binding upon and shall inure to the benefit of the parities hereto, their respective heirs, executors, administrators, devises, personal representatives, successors, and assigns.

25. **Headings.** The headings and captions contained herein are inserted for convenient reference only, and shall not

be deemed to construe or limit the paragraphs to which they apply.

26. **Attorney Approval Contingency.** This Agreement is subject to the written disapproval ("Notice of Disapproval") by the Purchaser's attorney within five days from the date Purchaser delivers to Seller the Agreement executed by Purchaser. The Notice of Disapproval must include the specific objections and proposed modifications of this Agreement; provided that in no event shall the attorney be entitled to object to or propose modifications to the sales price, broker's compensation, date or timing, or any monetary provision. IN THE EVENT THE NOTICE OF DISAPPROVAL IS NOT SUBMITTED TO SELLER WITHIN SAID TIME PERIOD, THIS ATTORNEY APPROVAL CONTINGENCY SHALL BE DEEMED TO HAVE BEEN WAIVED BY PURCHASER, AND THIS AGREEMENT SHALL REMAIN IN FULL FORCE AND EFFECT WITHOUT THIS CONTINGENCY. If the Notice of Disapproval is timely given by Purchaser's attorney, and within 14 days of the Purchaser's delivery of this Agreement to Seller, it becomes evident that the parties cannot reach agreement on the specific objections identified in the Notice of Disapproval, then this Agreement shall become null and void and all monies paid by Purchaser shall be refunded.

27. **Heating Cost Disclosure Information.** Purchaser acknowledges the receipt, prior to the execution of this Agreement, of the Heating Cost Disclosure Form issued in accordance with the Heating Cost Disclosure Ordinance of the City of Chicago.

28. **Riders.** The following Rider(s) are hereby incorporated into and made part of this contract: Rider(s) _____, _____, _____, and _____.

29. **Entire Agreement.** All negotiations, dealings, correspondence, and memoranda between the parties hereto are merged into the Agreement, which constitutes the entire agreement between Purchaser and Seller. NO REPRESENTATIONS, WARRANTIES, UNDERTAKING, OR PROMISES, WHETHER WRITTEN OR ORAL, EXPRESSED OR IMPLIED, CAN BE MADE OR HAVE BEEN MADE BY SELLER OR PURCHASER OR THEIR RESPECTIVE AGENTS, OFFICERS OR EMPLOYEES, UNLESS EXPRESSLY STATED HEREIN OR IN THE WARRANTY AGREEMENT, AS HEREINAFTER DEFINED, OR UNLESS MUTUALLY AGREED UPON IN WRITING BY THE PARTIES HERETO.

30. **Survival.** All representations and warranties of the parties shall be deemed to survive the Closing.

31. **Definition of Terms.** All terms used herein, if defined in the Declaration, shall have the same meanings as in the Declaration, unless specifically defined otherwise in this Agreement.

32. **Partial Invalidity.** The invalidity of any of the provisions of this Agreement shall not affect or impair the validity or enforceability of the remainder of this Agreement.

33. **RESPA.** Seller and Purchaser shall comply with all of the Purchaser's lender's requirements, if any, for disclosure under the Real Estate Settlement Procedural Act of 1974, as amended from time to time.

34. **Joint and Several Obligations.** If Purchaser is more than one person, then the obligations of Purchaser hereunder are joint and several.

I (WE), AS PURCHASER(S), HAVE READ AND DO UNDERSTAND THIS DOCUMENT, AND I (WE) HAVE HAD AN OPPORTUNITY TO SEEK PROFESSIONAL ADVICE CONCERNING ITS CONTENTS AND LEGAL

IMPLICATIONS, AND AFTER SO DOING, VOLUN-
TARILY EXECUTE THIS AGREEMENT AS MY (OUR)
FREE AND VOLUNTARY ACT

PURCHASER   **SELLER**
_____   ABC Management, Inc.,
_____   an Illinois corporation

Date Executed by Purchaser: _____
By: _____
Authorized Signatory
Purchaser's Social Security Number(s):

_____

Date Executed by Seller: ___ _____
Seller's Contact Person: Michael H. Zaransky
Phone number: (847) 562-1700
Fax number: (847) 714-1515
Email: _mhz@primepropertyinvestors.com_

Purchaser's Attorney: **Seller's Attorney:**

_____   _____
Name

_____   _____
Street Address

_____   _____
City, State, Zip Code

_____   _____
Fax Number

_____   _____
Email Address

_____   _____

EXHIBIT A

TO
12234 MAIN STREET
CONDOMINIUM PURCHASE AGREEMENT
PERSONAL PROPERTY TO BE DELIVERED AT CLOSING:

1. _____

2. _____

3. _____

4. _____

5. _____

6. _____

7. _____

8. _____

9. _____

10. _____

EXHIBIT B

TO
12234 MAIN STREET
CONDOMINIUM PURCHASE AGREEMENT
COPY OF FLOOR PLAN OF THE PURCHASED UNIT

EXHIBIT C

TO
12234 MAIN STREET
CONDOMINIUM PURCHASE AGREEMENT
CERTIFICATE OF LIMITED WARRANTY

Purchased Unit #:
Purchaser:
Purchase Agreement Date:
Closing Date:

ABC Management, Inc., an Illinois corporation, ("Warrantor") warrants the Purchased Unit in 12234 Main Street Condominium against latent defects in the Purchased Unit arising out of faulty workmanship or material for a period ("Warranty Period") of one year from Closing, subject to the terms and condition set forth herein. Warrantor's obligation under this warranty shall be limited to repair or replacement, at its option, of the faulty workmanship or material within a reasonable time after receipt of written notice from Purchaser. All work shall be performed during normal business hours.

The terms used in this Certificate of Limited Warranty, which are defined in the above-referenced Purchase Agreement between ABC Management, Inc., an Illinois corporation, and Purchaser shall have the same meaning herein as in the Purchase Agreement.

THIS WARRANTY IS DELIVERED PURSUANT TO PARAGRAPH 9 OF THE PURCHASE AGREEMENT, IS IN LIEU OF ALL OTHER WARRANTIES OF WARRANTOR, EXPRESS OR IMPLIED (INCLUDING WITHOUT LIMITATION ANY IMPLIED WARRANTY OF MERCHANTABILITY, HABITABILITY, OR FITNESS FOR A PARTICULAR PURPOSE), AND INDURES ONLY TO THE BENEFIT OF THE PREVIOUSLY-REFERENCED PUR-

CHASER AND NOT ANY SUCCESSOR, ASSIGNEE OR GRANTEE OR PURCHASER.

AS TO ANY PERSONAL PROPERTY, AND AS TO ANY CONSUMER PRODUCT (AS THAT TERM MAY BE DEFINED UNDER APPLICABLE FEDERAL, STATE OR LOCAL LAWS, OR THEIR IMPLEMENTING REGULATIONS) WHICH MAY BE CONTAINED IN THE PURCHASED UNIT, SELLER AND WARRANTOR NEITHER MAKE NOR ADOPT ANY WARRANTY WHATSOEVER, AND SPECIFICALLY EXCLUDE EXPRESS OR IMPLIED WARRANTIES OF ANY NATURE, INCLUDING ANY IMPLIED WARRANTY OF MERCHANTABILITY, SUITABILITY OR FITNESS FOR A PARTICULAR PURPOSE.

This warranty is subject to the following terms, conditions, and exclusions, all of which are an integral part hereof.

1. **Warranty Exclusions.** The following exclusions and limitations apply to Warrantor's warranty obligations:

   a) Defects in Finishes (hereinafter defined) not specifically noted on the punch list prepared prior to closing are excluded from this limited warranty. "Finishes" include, but are not limited to, laminated surfaces (countertops), cabinets, ceramic tile, stone surfaces, vinyl surfaces, composite surfaces, glass surfaces, metal surfaces, fixtures (bathtubs, showers, sinks, light fixtures, appliances), surfaces, screens, carpeting, or painted or stain-finished surfaces (walls, ceilings, stairs, doors, trim, woodwork, wood flooring, siding, soffits, fascia).

   b) Faucet leaks, toilet adjustments, door and doorframe adjustments, window and window-frame adjustments, and floor and wall tile grouting are covered for a period of 60 days after the Closing. Thereafter, any repairs or corrections are the responsibility of the Purchaser.

c)   Nail or screw pops or cracks in the walls and ceilings are not covered by this warranty, because such
conditions do not result from faulty workmanship
or defective materials but are the result of natural
shrinkage and drying out of building materials, or
of normal settlement of the building, wind loads, or
other normal movement of the building components.
If abnormal conditions (as determined by Warrantor)
exist with respect to these items, Warrantor will correct such conditions, but only once, within a reasonable time. Warrantor will not be liable for repainting,
wallpapering, or refinishing any repaired areas.

d)   This warranty does not cover ordinary wear and tear,
or damage due to misuse or neglect, negligence or
failure to provide proper maintenance. This warranty
does not cover items which have been modified or
repaired by anyone other than Seller or any items
which are installed or constructed pursuant to a separate contract or agreement between the Purchaser
and any party other than Warrantor.

e)   This warranty does not cover damage arising from
leaks or water infiltration at perimeter walls or any
defects in the Common Elements. This warranty does
not cover the Common Elements.

f)   This warranty does not cover heating and cooling
output variations from room to room or, in multiple
level units, from floor to floor.

g)   This warranty specifically excludes any incidental
and consequential damages caused by any defect or
breach of warranty.

h)   For the purpose of this warranty, "latent defects" are
limited to those defects which are not apparent at
the time of the preparation of the Inspection Report
but become apparent, and written notice of which is

given to Warrantor, prior to expiration of the Warranty Period.

2. **Manufacturers' Warranties.** Certain personal property and equipment within the Purchased Unit are supplied with manufacturers' instructions and warranties. It is recommended that the manufacturers' instruction pamphlets be read and followed. Similarly, sealed insulating glasses on window and door units are covered by limited manufacturer warranties. Warrantor is not a warrantor under, and does not adopt, such manufacturers' warranties. In the event of defects in such products, purchaser should contact the manufacturer directly. Warrantor is not responsible for the performance of any manufacturer under its warranty.

3. **Other Items.** No actions taken by Warrantor to correct defects shall extend the warranty beyond the warranty period. No representative of Warrantor has the authority to expand the scope of or extend the duration of this warranty or to make agreements with respect hereto. Warrantor shall not be obligated to remedy any defects where otherwise required pursuant to this warranty unless and until Purchaser notifies Warrantor in writing of the defect and then only if such notification is made prior to the expiation of the Warranty Period. To assist Seller in the administration of warranty work purchaser agrees to confirm satisfactory completion of such work upon request. This warranty shall be null and void as to any particular defect if Purchaser performs repairs to the Purchased Unit in respect to such defect without receiving the prior written consent of Warrantor. This warranty is not assignable and any attempted assignment shall render it null and void.

4. **Architect's Decision.** In the event of any dispute arising hereunder as to the existence of any defect, which dispute is not resolved by Warrantor and Purchaser, such dispute

shall be submitted to and resolved by the architectural firm of Edward P. Kestin & Associates, the architect for the Property, based upon customary trade standards or tolerances, this Warranty and the Purchase Agreement. Said Architects' decision shall be final and binding upon the parties. The fees for said architectural firm incurred in resolving any such disputes shall be paid by the party against whom the decision is render.

5. **Notices.** Any notices hereunder shall be personally delivered or sent by certified or registered mail, return receipt requested, addressed to:

If to Warrantor:

ABC Management, Inc.

c/o Prime Property Investors, Ltd.

1234 Any Street, Suite 506

Any Town, Illinois 99999

If to Purchase, to the address of the Purchased Unit.

Any notice mailed as aforesaid shall be deemed received three business days after deposit in the United States mail. Notice of changes of address for receipt of notices shall be sent in the manner set forth in the Paragraph 5.

ABC Management, Inc.,

An Illinois corporation,

By: _____

Authorized Signatory

PURCHASER ACKNOWLEDGES THAT HE OR SHE IS (THEY ARE) PURCHASING THE UNIT OWNERSHIP WITHOUT ANY WARRANTY OF REPRESENTATION OF ANY KIND, EXPRESS OR IMPLIED, BY SELLER OR ANY OFFICER, EMPLOYEE, AGENT, BROKER, OR OTHER REPRESENTATIVE OF SELLER EXCEPT FOR THE LIMITED WARRANTY SET FORTH IN THIS CERTIFICATE OF WARRANTY.

Purchaser(s):

_____

_____

RIDER A

This Rider is incorporated into and made a part of that certain Condominium Purchase Agreement (the "Agreement"), dated _____, 20__, by and between _____ ("Purchaser") and ABC Management, Inc.

R-1 All capitalized terms used in this Rider shall have the same meanings as said terms have in the Agreement. In the event of any conflict between the provisions of the Agreement and the provisions of the Rider, the provisions of this Rider shall govern.

R-2 a) In the event that Seller and Purchaser shall execute an Extra Order, the cost of the Extras that are the subject of such Extra Order shall be added to the Purchase Price and shall be paid to Seller in accordance with the provisions of the following subparagraph R-2(b).

b) In the event that Purchaser and Seller shall execute an Extra Order with respect to any Extra, then, concurrently with the execution by Purchaser and Seller of such Extra Order, Purchaser shall pay to Seller 100 percent of the cost of the Extras that are the subject of such Extra Order.

c) No payments for Extras will be held in escrow. All such payments may be used by Seller to pay for such Extras.

d) If the Closing contemplated by this Agreement shall not occur for any reason other than a default by Seller under this Agreement, then, subject to the provisions of Paragraph 18(a) of this Agreement, Seller shall be entitled to retain as its sole and absolute property all sums paid by Purchaser to Seller for such Extras pursuant to the terms of any Extra Orders executed by Purchaser and Seller.

R-3 Purchaser hereby acknowledges that Seller may maintain one or more models of the residential units to be constructed in the Building, and that said models may contain items, special features and/or upgrades that are not included in the Purchase Price and that will not be contained in the Residential Unit. Such items, special features and/or upgrades include, without limitation, all of the following contained in the models: all furniture, furnishings, decorations, accessories, drapes, verticals, blinds or other window treatments, upgraded carpeting and floor coverings, wall coverings, paneling and other wall treatments, intercoms, kitchen accessories, chandeliers, and any other type of hanging fixtures, upgraded fixture and special lighting effects, mirrors and extra or upgraded appliances.

Executed this _____ day of _____, 20__.

PURCHASER   **SELLER**

_____   ABC Management, Inc.

_____   an Illinois corporation

By: _____

Authorized Signatory

10

LIST OF TYPICAL PHYSICAL ENHANCEMENT IMPROVEMENTS FOR A GUT REHAB CONDOMINIUM CONVERSION

List of finishes provided in condominium unit:

- Individual central heat and air-conditioning
- All new red oak select hardwood floors
- Imported ceramic tile in bathroom floor and shower wall
- New stainless kitchen appliances include: refrigerator, dishwasher, stove with oven, microwave with hood, and garbage disposal
- Stainless steel under-mount kitchen sink
- All new Moen faucets
- All new important kitchen cabinets and island
- Granite kitchen countertops
- Granite top with Kohler under-mount sink in bathroom
- Important vanity cabinet in bathroom
- New Kohler bathtub and toilet
- Washer-dryer hook-up and unit owner's owned or new washer-dryer in lower-level common area

- Recessed can lighting
- Solid core interior room entry doors
- Deluxe trim
- Private deck

11

SAMPLE INCOME AND EXPENSE PROJECTION FOR INCOME-PRODUCING INVESTMENT RENTAL PROPERTY

Annualized Income and Expense Statement

Income	
Gross rental income	$235,260
Laundry and misc.	$1,800
Gross annual income potential	$237,060
Less vacancy and collection loss (3%)	$7,058
Effective gross annual income	*$230,002*
Expenses	
Real estate taxes	$36,351
Insurance	$11,604
Advertising	$3,400
Cleaning and maintenance	$3,900
Repairs and supplies	$4,000
Utilities	$32,000
Landscape and snow removal	$1,900
Scavenger	$1,300
Total expenses	*($94,455)*
Net operating income	*$135,547*

SAMPLE LETTER TO A HOMEOWNER IN FORECLOSURE SEEKING TO PURCHASE A HOME PRIOR TO A FORECLOSURE AUCTION

1234 Main Street
Chicago, IL 60640
February 22, 2007

Dear Mr. and Mrs. Public:

I wish to purchase your home for all cash in a quick transaction with no contingencies. I am a real estate broker and want to purchase your property directly with no commission.

You'll walk away from the closing, to be scheduled as soon as you wish, with all mortgages and liens paid in full and excess cash equity to you.

Please contact me immediately to confidentially discuss a transaction.

Very truly yours,
Michael H. Zaransky
CEO

P.S. I have vast experience and resources and can move very rapidly to purchase your home, pay off your mortgage, and have you walk away with cash!

SAMPLE LETTER OF INTENT FOR A NET-LEASED COMMERCIAL OR RETAIL PROPERTY

LETTER OF INTENT

September 21, 2006
Mr. Bruce A. Broker
ABC Brokerage
One Town Square
Any Town, USA
Re: Starbucks Coffee

Dear Bruce:

This letter of intent will evidence the intent of a to-be-formed LLC affiliated with our company (the "Buyer") to enter into a contract of purchase with the Owner of Record (the "Seller") for the purchase by Buyer of the real estate property commonly known as Starbucks Coffee, 123 Main Street (the "Property"). The purchase by Buyer shall be on the terms and subject to the conditions set forth below:

1. At the closing of the transaction (the Closing), Seller shall sell the property to Buyer free and clear of all liens,

encumbrances, claims or interests of any kind other than existing leases and other exceptions permitted as set forth in the legally binding, written agreement to be negotiated and entered into by Buyer and Seller.

2. In consideration of the sale and transfer of the property, Buyer shall pay the Seller the total sum of **$1,500,000,** adjusted for prorations, at closing, for rent, and other similar items (the "Purchase Price").

3. The purchase price shall be payable with an earnest money deposit, to bear interest for the benefit of Buyer of the sum of $50,000 due upon execution of the execution of a binding contract for purchase, and the $1,450,000 balance, plus or minus prorations, payable to Seller at closing.

4. The obligation of Buyer to purchase the property is conditioned upon the performance by Buyer of such inspections as Buyer deems appropriate or necessary including, but not limited to, a feasibility study, financial due diligence, environmental, structural, and mechanical inspections of the land and improvements comprising the Property. Buyer shall complete all such inspections and due diligence within 30 days of execution of a legally binding agreement. If Buyer finds the property to be unsatisfactory to Buyer for any or no reason, prior to the expiration of the inspection and due-diligence period, Buyer shall, at its option declare the contract void and all earnest money deposited herein shall be immediately returned to the Buyer. Seller shall fully cooperate with Buyer in connection with such inspections and allow Buyer access, upon reasonable notice, to the property, and will provide Buyer with any information Buyer deems necessary or desirable in connection with such inspections. Seller will provide a copy of the proposed Starbucks Coffee leases in effect for the property, with all riders and modifications, upon execution of this letter of intent.

5. Buyer and Seller agree to use their best efforts to (a) enter a legally binding contract of purchase agreement within ten days after acceptance of this letter of intent, and (b) close the transaction contemplated hereby upon completion and final occupancy, and commencement of the rental obligation, of the premises by Starbucks Coffee.

6. The Buyer and Seller agree that this letter of intent outlines the terms and conditions upon which Buyer will enter a legally binding agreement to purchase the Property from Seller and that the entering of such agreement is specifically conditioned upon the completion of the inspections required under number 4 above, to the satisfaction of the Buyer. The final legally binding agreement to purchase and all sale documents must be in a form acceptable to both Buyer and Seller, and their respective legal counsel.

Very truly yours,
Michael H. ZaranskyBarbara J. Gaffen
Co-CEOCo-CEO

MHZ: tlb

THIS LETTER OF INTENT IS VOID AND WITHDRAWN IF NOT ACCEPTED ON OR BEFORE SEPTEMBER 22, 2006

Acknowledged and Agreed To:

Seller: _____

Date: _____

Required Disclosure: Michael H. Zaransky, Barbara J. Gaffen, and Prime Property Investors, Ltd. are licensed Real Estate Brokers in the State of Illinois.

14

SAMPLE SINGLE-FAMILY HOME CONSTRUCTION RENOVATION PLAN

Construction Renovation Plan

The property is a vintage-style three-story plus basement, Victorian single-family home located in the Lincoln Square neighborhood. The property currently consists of ten large rooms with four bedrooms and two full baths and is located on an oversized 37 × 125 foot lot. Purchase price will be $444,000. The single-family home will be gut rehabbed and turned into an updated home with in excess of 4,000 square feet of living area plus a rear deck, front porch, and new two-and-a-half-car garage.

The construction cost for the project is anticipated to be $225,000. The project will take from four to five months to complete. Upon completion, based upon comparable property sales, the as-completed fair market value of the house is anticipated to be in excess $800,000. Improvements include:

- Complete new home exterior siding and complete new tear-off roof
- Complete new double-hung low-e double-pane windows
- Complete new open front porch and new rear wood deck

- New two-and-a-half-car garage and landscaping
- Interior new and refinished hardwood floors throughout house
- New master bath suite and redone existing bathrooms with new ceramic tile and plumbing fixtures
- New kitchen cabinets, stainless steel appliances, and granite counter tops
- Build out of lower-level basement with drywall, bathroom, and additional office/bedroom area
- All new HVAC central air and heat system, new plumbing system, upgraded electrical service
- New room configurations, sunroom on master suite, storage areas, and stairwells to maximize open space with new drywall and trim throughout home
- New interior prehung doors and moldings
- Deluxe paint and stain finishing throughout

15

MARKETING PAGE FOR A REPOSITIONED SINGLE-TENANT, NET-LEASED OFFICE BUILDING (FROM A RESALE MARKETING PACKAGE)

FOR SALE

United States Post Office
Olympia Fields, Illinois
Secure Net Lease to U.S. Government
Armchair Investment in Prime Location

This unique investment opportunity offers the stable cash flow and security associated with the ownership of a U.S. government guaranteed-rent obligation along with the potential for substantial appreciation in the underlying real estate value.

The Olympia Fields Post Office, located in downtown Olympia Fields, adjacent to the Metra Commuter Train Station and newer luxury home developments, is leased to the U.S. Postal Service on a current five-year term until August, 2005. Upon expiration, the lessee has the option to renew the lease for an additional five-year term at an increased rental rate. Under the long-term net lease, the Postal Service is responsible for the reimbursement of the real estate taxes on the property as additional rent.

The well-located site consists of 20,040 square feet encompassing a rarely available half-acre of land in the growing south suburban Chicago community of Olympia Fields. The building improvements, built to suit for the U.S. Postal Service, consists of a one-story office structure containing 2,852 square feet, a rear loading dock, paved off-street parking, and a quaint colonial appearance.

Based on the current income and expense results of operation, the property is offered at an attractive 8 percent capitalization rate providing the investor with a no-risk immediate cash-on-cash return on a well-located, highly secure, net-lease investment. The building is offered at below-replacement cost. Upon renewal at the end of the current term, at the option year rent rate, the investor will receive an 8.8 percent cash-on-cash return.

The property seller is a licensed Illinois Real Estate Broker affiliated firm and the offering brokers have an ownership interest in the subject property.

Contact:
Prime Property Investors, Ltd.
Michael H. Zaransky or Barbara J. Gaffen
(847) 562-1800

16

SAMPLE RETURN ANALYSIS FOR THE POTENTIAL PURCHASE OF A HOTEL CONDOMINIUM UNIT

STUDIO GUEST ROOM PROJECTED ANNUAL INCOME AND RETURN ON INVESTMENT

- Studio guest room purchase price including furniture and fixtures: $461,000
- Amount financed 80 percent: $369,000
- Equity invested: $92,000
- Current studio guest room 5-star hotel per-night room rate: $430
- Hotel service expense fee $55 per room night stay
- 80 percent mortgage at 6 percent interest only

	70% Occupancy Commercial RE Tax	85% Occupancy Residential RE Tax
Annual income	*$109,865*	*$133,407*
Annual expenses		
Condominium assessments	$12,564	$12,564
Hotel fixed expenses	$11,904	$11,904
Hotel per night service fees	$14,052	$17,064
R.E. taxes	$18,120	$9,220
Total expenses before mortgage	*$56,650*	*$50,752*
Net operating income	*$53,215*	*$82,655*
Annual debt service	$22,140	$22,140
Net annual cash flow	*$31,075*	*$60,515*
Annual return on equity	*33.77%*	*65.77%*

SINGLE-FAMILY HOME REHAB PROJECT PRO FORMA PROFIT STATEMENT

Repair Construction-Improvements to be made

MISC
Building permits
Plumber
Carpenter

EXTERIOR
New roof
Paint front porch
Windows/all including front bay vinyl
Back sliding glass door/screens
Landscaping
Storm door
Dumpster

INTERIOR
Cleanup and demo
Refinish hardwood

Ceramic tile as needed
Carpet as needed
Interior paint
Kitchen design
Kitchen cabinets
Stainless steel appliances
Washer/dryer
Granite
New toilets
New vanities
Faucets
Tub and tile glaze bathroom
Ceramic in pink bathroom
Cleaning
Carpet

Purchase price	285,000
Improvement cost	40,000
Soft costs	+ 20,000
Purchase price and costs	345,000
Anticipated as-improved net value	– 395,000
Anticipated profit	**50,000**

Michael H. Zaransky is a graduate of the University of Illinois at Champaign Urbana as a James Scholar, as well as Northwestern University School of Law. He has been a licensed real estate broker in the State of Illinois since 1979. He's a founder and co-CEO of Northbrook, Illinois-based Prime Property Investors, Ltd. His firm has received numerous awards and industry recognition for its real estate projects and was named as one of the 50 best companies in residential construction and development to work for by the national publication *Professional Builder*. He has published numerous articles on the subject of real estate investment.

Zaransky has spoken to many professional groups and moderated numerous panel discussions regarding real estate investment. He has been quoted in local and national publications on the subject and is recognized as a leader in the field in the Chicago area.

Active in a large number of real estate trade organizations, Zaransky has built an extensive network of real estate professionals. He currently serves as a member of the Board of Directors and Executive Committee of the Chicago Association of REALTORS® and is the past chairman of the Association's Commercial and Investment Division. He has written a monthly column in *The Chicago Realtor* and founded the first-ever citywide Commercial and Investment Real Estate Awards dinner in Chicago.

Zaransky's professional affiliations include:

- National Apartment Association
- Chicago Association of REALTORS®
- National Association of REALTORS®

- National Multi-Housing Council
- National Association of Home Builders
- University of Illinois Alumni Association
- Northwestern University Alumni Association
- Young Presidents Organization Alumni (YPO)

A

Acceptance
  letter of intent, 140, 141, 193
  purchase agreement, 143, 144, 156
  timeline, 171
Add-ons, 160
After-purchase repositioning, 94-95
Americans with Disabilities Act, 125
Apartment building
  condominium conversion, 98-101
  consumer demand, 89-90
  economic enhancements, 94-96
  interior enhancements, 7-8, 10, 21
  letter of intent, 138-41
  neighborhood, 96-98
  niche opportunities, 101-3
  physical enhancements, 90-93
  resale marketing cover sheet, 136-37
  trends, 17-18, 65
Apartment and commercial property owners' association, 63
As-completed value, 68-69, 70
Assignment, 168
Attorney approval contingency, 175
Aurora (Illinois), 90-93

B

Bank of America, 113
Bank financing, 52-54
Bathrooms, 10, 79-80
Binding agreement, 174
Bond-type leases, 112
Bottom line, 26-27, 69-70
Broker, 168-69
Brokerage accounts, 35
Business cycle, 65-66

C

Cash flow
  increase, 18-19
  operating expenses and, 23-26
  opportunities, 59-60
  property value and, 26-27
Certificate of limited warranty, 180-86
Chamber of Commerce, 62
Chase Bank, 113
Chicago Association of REALTORS, 78
Chicagoland Apartment Association, 93
Closing, 162-65
Commercial real estate brokerage company, 60
Commission, 139
Competitive property risk, 123-24
Condominium
  association, 148-50
  cosmetic rehab, 84-85
  documents, 157-59

hotel, 117-19, 198-99
  interior enhancement, 7-8
  office, 108-9, 110
  project cost/benefit, 133-34
Condominium conversion
  added-value with, 98-101
  cosmetic rehab project, 108-10
  gut rehab, 187-88
  net profit projection, 151-52
  physical enhancement improvements, 187-88
  profit-and-loss comparison sheet, 133-34
  unit purchase agreement, 153-86
Construction management
  field work, 14
  general contractor, 11-14
  insurance, 12-13
  licensing, 12
  permits, 13
  purchase agreement provision, 154-55
  renovation plan, 194-95
  trade associations, 14-15
Cosmetic rehab
  condominium, 84-88, 108-10
  exterior, 5-6
  interior, 7-10
  single-family home, 80-84
Credit card, 35-36
Credibility, 62-64
Curb appeal, 5
CVS, 113

D

Debt financing
  access to, 50
  aggressive use of, 47-48
  cautions, 49
  lender relations, 49-52
  mortgage brokers, 56-57
  personal guarantees, 54-55
  sources of, 52-54, 57-58
Default provisions, 169-70
Deficiency, 54-55
Direct mail, 61
Due-diligence
  contingency period, 70-72
  hotel condominium, 118
  investigations, 70
  letter of intent provisions,
    139-40
  sales contract rider, 143
  student housing, 103,
    145-47

E

Earnest money, 139
Economic enhancements,
  94-96
Emerging neighborhoods,
  15-18
Employment factors, 122
Engineering report, 6-7
Equity capital
  availability, 45
  definition of, 32-34
  friends/relatives, 39-40
  hard money, 33
  institutional partners,
    43-45
  joint ventures, 40-41
  partnership arrangements,
    33-34, 36-38
  sources of, 34-36, 38-45
  syndication, 41-43

Excess costs, 9
Exhibits, 178-86
Exterior improvements, 4-7
External economic factors,
  62-67
Extras, 160

F

Fair market value, 19, 22-23
Feasibility inspection contingency clause. 71
Feasibility period, 70-72
Final evaluation, 72
Financing
  access, 50
  condominium conversion,
    101
  lender relations, 49-52
  mistakes, 92-93
  personal guarantee, 54-55
  purchase agreement
    provisions, 171-74
  sources, 52-54, 57-58
Floor plan, 179
Foreclosure
  letter to homeowner, 190
  properties, 79
Friends, 39-40

G

Gaffen, Barbara, 37
Gender, 171
General contractor, 11-13
General economic conditions,
  122
Gold Coast neighborhood,
  84-85
Good Neighbor Award, 86
Government regulation, 125
Gross income
  operating expenses and,
    23-25
  rental rates and, 22-23

Gross profit potential, 69
Gut rehab
  condominium conversion
    project, 187-88
  single-family home project,
    85-87

H

Hard money, 33
Hardwood floors, 8-9
Headings/captions, 174-75
Heating cost disclosure, 175
High-growth neighborhood,
  107-10
Home equity loan, 34
Hotel condominium, 117-19,
  198-99
Hotel properties, 116-19

I

Income and expense projection, 189
Industrial warehouse, 8
Institutional partners, 43-45
Insurance
  expense, 24
  as financing source, 35, 58
  general contractor, 11-13
Interest rates, 123
Interior improvements, 4, 7-10
Introduction letters, 63
Investment
  cashing in, 129
  economic conditions, 122
  external factors, 62-67
  illiquidity of, 126
  opportunities, x-xi
  locating property, 59-62
  property types, 128
  risk factors, 121-26
  viability of, 29-30

J

Joint and several obligation, 176-77
Joint venture, 40-41

K

Kitchen upgrades, 10, 79-80

L

Lender relationships, 49-52
Letter of intent
    apartment building, 138-41
    due-diligence provisions, 139-40
    net-leased property, 191-93
    preparation, 67, 70
Leverage, 49-50
Licensing requirements, 12
Life insurance
    company as financing source, 58
    loans against, 35
Limited liability company, 41, 43
Limited partnership, 41
Limited warranty, 161, 180-86
Lincoln Square neighborhood, 86-87
Line of credit, 34-35
Long-term lease, 111-12

M

Maintenance costs, 24
Management expense, 23
Manufacturing business, xi-xii
Market
    factors, 64-67
    rents, 22-23
    trends, 17-18
Material destruction, 170-71

M

Mechanical enhancements, 6-7, 10
Merriville (Indiana), 95-96
Mixed-use property, 107-10
Momentum, 63-64
Mortgage brokers, 56-57
Multifamily apartment building
    condo conversions, 98-101
    consumer demand, 89-90
    economic enhancements, 94-96
    neighborhood wave, 96-98
    niche opportunities, 101-3
    physical enhancements, 90-93

N

National Association of Home Builders, 15
National Association of REALTORS, 60
National Multi Housing Council, 18
National tenant, 111-12
Neighborhood wave, 15-16, 96-98
Net-leased property
    letter of intent, 191-93
    marketing package page, 196-97
    national tenant, 111-13
Net operating income
    bottom-line and, 26-27
    enhancements, 18-19
    estimates, 68
    increase, 18-19
    operating expenses and, 23-26
    property value and, 26-27
Net profit, 69, 151-52
Networking, 62
No mortgage contingency, 50, 51
Notices, 99-100, 169

O

Occupancy, 165-67
Office condominiums, 108-9, 110
Operating expense
    control of, 125
    insurance, 24
    payroll, 23
    projected, 68
    property values and, 25-26
    reduction of, 23-25
    repair/maintenance, 24
    utilities, 24-25
Operating partners, 36, 55

P

Parking issues, 110
Partial invalidity, 176
Partnership arrangement, 33-34, 36-38
Passive investors, 55
Payroll, 23
Permits, 13
Personal guarantees, 54-55
    Personal property listing, 178
    purchase agreement provisions, 161-62
Physical enhancement
    case study, 90-93
    condo conversion, 187-88
    exterior improvements, 4-7
    importance of, 3-4
    interior improvements, 4, 7-10
Possession, 165-67
Price-adjustments, 71-72
Principals, 61-62
Profit-and-loss comparison sheet, 133-34
Profit formula, 8
Pro forma profit statement, 200-201

roperty
    enhancement areas, 1-2
    flipping, 77
    management company, 61
    owners, 66, 135
    profitability, 68-70
    purchase offers, 50-51
    trends, 15-18
Public transportation, 16-17
Purchase agreement, 153-86
Purchase price, 139, 155-57

R

Ravenswood neighborhood,
    108-10
Real estate cycle, 65-66
Real Estate Settlement Proce-
    dures Act, 176
Real estate tax, 25
Recordation, 168
Recourse financing, 54-55
Refinance, 129
Reflagging, 116-17
Relatives, 39-40
Rent
    delinquency, 124
    increases, 22-23
    subsidy, 94
Rental property
    income and expense pro-
        jection, 189
    residential, 123
Repairs, 24
Resale market, 129
Resale marketing package,
    cover sheet, 136-37
Research, 18
Retail properties, 115, 191-93
Return analysis, 198-99
Rider
    purchase agreement, 175,
        185-86
    sales contract, 142-44

Rogers Park neighborhood,
    96-98
Roof, 6, 7

S

Sales contract rider, 142-44
Self-storage property, 8
Seller's easement, 167-68
Single-family home
    buying right, 78-85
    complete gut rehab, 85-87
    construction renovation
        plan, 194-95
    cosmetic rehab, 80-84
    kitchen/bath upgrades,
        79-80
    locating, 79
    possibilities, 77-78
    pro forma profit state-
        ment, 200-201
Soft costs, 8, 69
Starbucks, 113
Starbucks factor, 17
Strategic alliance, 40-41
Structural changes, 6-7, 10
Student housing
    due-diligence checklist,
        145-47
    market, 101-3
    sales contract rider, 142-44
Subcontractors, 14
Survival, 176
Syndication, 41-43

T

Targeted property
    as-completed value, 68-69
    bottom line, 69-70
    due-diligence contingency
        period, 70-72
    external market factors,
        64-67

feasibility period, 70-72
    final evaluation, 72
    ideal attributes, 72-73
    letter of intent, 67, 70
    letter to owners, 135
    NOI estimates, 68
    number crunching, 67-72
    price-adjustments, 71-72
    third party-investigative
        reports, 70
Taxes, 25
Tenant base, 24
Terrorist risk, 126
Third-party investigative
    reports, 70
Title conveyance, 159
Total direct improved cost, 69
Trade associations, 14-15
Triple-net leased property, 111
Trump International Hotel,
    118-19

U

Under-market rents, 94
Urban Land Institute, 18
Urban trend, 16-17
U.S. Postal System, 112
Utility costs, 24-25

V

Vacancy-and-collection loss, 68
Vacant space, 124-25
Value-added techniques
    cash flow, 18-19
    categories, 1-2
    condo conversion, 98-101
    construction business
        knowledge, 11-15
    emerging neighborhoods,
        15-18
    hotel property, 116

net operating income,
    18-19
physical enhancement,
    3-10
property types for, 105
rent increases, 22
Vintage homes, 85-86
Vintage Property of the Year
    Award, 93

W

Walgreen's, 113
Warranty provisions, 161